.2016

The Illustrated Book of

SOUNDS

& THEIR SPELLING PATTERNS

The right-brained approach to teaching word structure in 20 minutes a day

For kindergarten
through adult

Sarah K Major, M.Ed.

CHILD1st
PUBLICATIONS LLC

For teaching resources for visual & other
right-brained learners, visit

www.child1st.com

The Illustrated Book of Sounds & Their Spelling Patterns, 2nd Edition

Grades: Kindergarten through adult

© 2010 Sarah K Major

ISBN: 978-0-9829873-0-8

Printed in the United States of America

All rights reserved. The reproduction of any part of this book for an entire school or school system or for commercial use is strictly prohibited. No form of this work may be reproduced, transmitted, or recorded without written permission from the publisher. The pages in this book bearing a copyright line may be reproduced for instructional or administrative use (not for resale).

To request more information regarding the copyright policy, contact:

Child1st Publications

800-881-0912 (phone)

888-886-1636 (fax)

info@child1st.com

www.child1st.com

THE ILLUSTRATED BOOK OF SOUNDS & THEIR SPELLING PATTERNS

There are a finite number of sounds that make up all the words in our language. With *The Illustrated Book of Sounds & Their Spelling Patterns*, students will learn to read/spell those sounds that are the building blocks of all words. *The Illustrated Book of Sounds & Their Spelling Patterns* replaces ineffective memorization of words, phonics rules, or decoding with kid-friendly, brain-friendly patterns and visuals. Students are engaged in listening to sounds, finding patterns, learning through cartoons and story bites. *The Illustrated Book of Sounds & Their Spelling Patterns* demystifies reading and spelling by giving students the tools they need to identify unknown, difficult words with ease.

The Illustrated Book of Sounds & Their Spelling Patterns has been tested from regular classrooms to resource and special education settings, from whole group to small group, and with children in grades one through middle school. *The Illustrated Book of Sounds & Their Spelling Patterns* empowers teachers and parents to provide differentiated instruction to every student regardless of their ability level.

The best news about *The Illustrated Book of Sounds & Their Spelling Patterns* is that it can be incorporated into any existing curriculum in 15-20 minutes a day in place of the spelling lesson; learning becomes fun and lasting, producing fluent readers. *The Illustrated Book of Sounds & Their Spelling Patterns* is also teacher-friendly. Once you are familiar with the approach, your work is done! Simply present each lesson, review 10-15 minutes for the next three days, then assess on the 5th day. This cycle is repeated as you progress through the book.

This book is a perfect companion to the Easy-for-Me™ Reading Program.

TABLE OF CONTENTS

Recommended Sequence of Lessons vii

Fundamentals ix

Finger mapping xi

Daily Routine xv

Sound Spellings and Their Keywords Chart xvi

Using Keywords Effectively xvii

Tracking Sheet & Teaching Notes xviii

    Unit 1:   Short A 1

    Unit 2:   Short E 3

    Unit 3:   Short I 6

    Unit 4:   Short O 9

    Unit 5:   Short U 13

    Unit 6:   Long A 16

    Unit 7:   Long E 20

    Unit 8:   Long I 25

    Unit 9:   Long O 28

    Unit 10: Long U 32

    Unit 11: Sh 33

    Unit 12: Th 35

    Unit 13: Ch 37

    Unit 14: Wh 39

    Unit 15: ōō 41

Unit 16:   oo 45

Unit 17:   oi & oy 47

Unit 18:   ou & ow 50

Unit 19:   ng, nk 53

Unit 20:   Y /long e/ & /long i/ 55

Unit 21:   /er/ 57

Unit 22:   /ar/ 62

Unit 23:   /air/ 65

Unit 24:   /ear/ 67

Unit 25:   /or/ 69

Unit 26:   C /s/ & G /j/ 73

Unit 27:   Double Consonants 77

Unit 28:   Schwa 80

Unit 29:   /F/ 81

Unit 30:   /G/ 84

Unit 31:   /K/ 85

Unit 32:   /L/ 87

Unit 33:   /M/ 91

Unit 34:   /N/ 92

Unit 35:   /R/ 93

Unit 36:   /S/ 96

Unit 37:   /T/ 98

Unit 38:   /Z/ 100

Unit 39:   OUGH 6 ways 101

Unit 40:   Past tense 103

Unit 41:   Plurals 106

Unit 42:   en 109

Unit 43:   ish, ize, & ist 110

Unit 44:   or & er 111

Unit 45:   ion & ian 112

Unit 46:   ture & sure 114

Unit 47:   cia, tia, & sia 115

Unit 48:   ate, ment, & ness 116

Unit 49:   ant, ent, & eer 117

Unit 50:   ary, ity, & ty 119

Unit 51:   ally, ly, & ward 121

Unit 52:   ous 122

Unit 53:   cious, tious, scious, & xious 123

Unit 54:   ious & eous 124

Unit 55:   Homophones 126

Y, W, V, P, B, D not included because the sounds of these consonants are not made with other letters. Ex: /B/ is always spelled either B or BB.

The only exception to this is the sound for /H/ which is spelled H and WH as in "who."

RECOMMENDED SEQUENCE OF LESSONS

This book is organized into units, each of which explores a particular sound and which contains words of varying levels of difficulty. Teacher/parent will select the **sound** they wish to teach and then choose the **level** in that unit that is appropriate for the students. However, a recommended sequence of lessons is provided so students are well prepared for each lesson. **Note:** Lessons 1-36 correspond roughly to 1st-2nd grades, Lessons 37-75 correspond roughly to grades 3-4, Lessons 76-103 corresponds roughly to grades 4-5, and finally, Lessons 104 and on are appropriate for Middle School. However, if a child is ready to move ahead, follow his lead. Young children are capable of far more than we think!

***Please study FUNDAMENTALS page ix, FINGERMAPPING page xi, and utilize TEACHING NOTES beginning on page xx.**

Recommended Sequence of Lessons

| 1............Unit 1, Level 1........Short a /ă/.........................p. 1 |
| 2............Unit 2, Level 1........Short e /ĕ/.........................p. 3 |
| 3............Unit 3, Level 1........Short i /ĭ/..........................p. 6 |
| 4............Unit 4, Level 1........Short o /ŏ/.........................p. 9 |
| 5............Unit 5, Level 1........Short u /ŭ/.........................p. 13 |
| 6............Unit 1, Level 2........Short a /ă/.........................p. 2 |
| 7............Unit 11, Level 1........sh, ce /sh/.......................p. 33 |
| 8............Unit 12, Level 1........th /th/.............................p. 35 |
| 9............Unit 13, Level 1........ch /ch/............................p. 37 |
| 10............Unit 2, Level 2........Short e /ĕ/.......................p. 4 |
| 11............Unit 3, Level 2........Short i /ĭ/........................p. 7 |
| 12............Unit 19, Level 1........ng and nk......................p. 53 |
| 13............Unit 4, Level 2........o, a /ŏ/...........................p. 10 |
| 14............Unit 6, Level 1........a-e /ā/...........................p. 16 |
| 15............Unit 6, Level 2........ey, ai, ay /ā/...................p. 17 |
| 16............Unit 7, Level 1........e, ee, e-e /ē/..................p. 20 |
| 17............Unit 20, Level 1........y /ī/ /ē/........................p. 55 |
| 18............Unit 8, Level 1........i, y /ī/............................p. 25 |
| 19............Unit 8, Level 2........ie, i-e /ī/........................p. 26 |
| 20............Unit 8, Level 3........igh, e-e, eigh, is, ais /ī/...p. 27 |
| 21............Unit 32, Level 1........l, ll, il /l/.......................p. 87 |
| 22............Unit 9, Level 1........o /ō/..............................p. 28 |
| 23............Unit 9, Level 2........oo, o-e /ō/.....................p. 29 |
| 24............Unit 9, Level 3........oa, ow /ō/.......................p. 30 |
| 25............Unit 10................u, u-e, ue, ew /ū/..........p. 32 |
| 26............Unit 15, Level 1........u, o, u-e /oo/.................p. 41 |
| 27............Unit 15, Level 2........ou, oo, oe, o-e /oo/........p. 42 |
| 28............Unit 16, Level 1........u, oo /oo/.....................p. 45 |
| 29............Unit 17, Level 1........oi, oy /oy/......................p. 47 |
| 30............Unit 18, Level 1........ou, ow /ow/....................p. 50 |
| 31............Unit 21, Level 1........ir, er, or /er/...................p. 57 |
| 32............Unit 21, Level 2........ir, ur /er/........................p. 58 |
| 33............Unit 22, Level 1........ar /ar/............................p. 62 |
| 34............Unit 22, Level 2........ar /ar/............................p. 63 |
| 35............Unit 31, Level 1........c, ck, k /k/.....................p. 85 |
| 36............Unit 31, Level 2........ck, ch, k, c /k/ qu...........p. 86 |
| 37............Unit 2, Level 3........ea, ai, ie /ĕ/....................p. 5 |
| 38............Unit 4, Level 3........a, aw /ŏ/.........................p. 11 |
| 39............Unit 5, Level 2........oe, o, u /ŭ/.....................p. 14 |
| 40............Unit 23, Level 1........air, eir, ere, are /air/.......p. 65 |
| 41............Unit 24, Level 1........ere, eer /ear/..................p. 67 |
| 42............Unit 24, Level 2........ear, ier /ear/...................p. 68 |
| 43............Unit 25, Level 1........or, ore /or/.....................p. 69 |
| 44............Unit 25, Level 2........or, ore /or/.....................p. 70 |
| 45............Unit 26, Level 1........ce /s/ ge, gi, gy /j/.........p. 73 |
| 46............Unit 26, Level 2........c(e), c(i) /s/ ge, dge /j/....p. 74 |
| 47............Unit 27, Level 1........Double consonants.........p. 77 |

| 48............Unit 27, Level 2........Double consonants.........p. 78 |
| 49............Unit 7, Level 2........y, ey, ee, ea /ē/..............p. 21 |
| 50............Unit 7, Level 3........ea /ē/.............................p. 22 |
| 51............Unit 9, Level 4........oe, ou, ough /ō/..............p. 31 |
| 52............Unit 12, Level 2........th /th/............................p. 36 |
| 53............Unit 13, Level 2........ch, tch /ch/.....................p. 38 |
| 54............Unit 14, Level 1........wh /wh/..........................p. 39 |
| 55............Unit 15, Level 3........ui, ew, ue, ough /oo/.......p. 43 |
| 56............Unit 16, Level 2........oul, oo /oo/....................p. 46 |
| 57............Unit 17, Level 2........oi, oy /oy/......................p. 48 |
| 58............Unit 18, Level 2........ou, ow /ow/....................p. 51 |
| 59............Unit 28................Sound of schwa /uh/......p. 80 |
| 60............Unit 19, Level 2........./ng/   nk /ngk/..............p. 54 |
| 61............Unit 20, Level 2........y /ē/..............................p. 56 |
| 62............Unit 21, Level 3........ur, or, ear, er /er/............p. 59 |
| 63............Unit 25, Level 3........ar, oor, our /or/..............p. 71 |
| 64............Unit 29, Level 2........ph, gh /f/........................p. 82 |
| 65............Unit 32, Level 2........le, al /l/...........................p. 88 |
| 66............Unit 35, Level 1........rh, wr /r/..........................p. 93 |
| 67............Unit 40, Level 1........ed /t/, /d/, /ed/................p. 103 |
| 68............Unit 40, Level 2........ed /t/, /d/, /ed/................p. 104 |
| 69............Unit 41, Level 1........Plurals: s and es.............p. 106 |
| 70............Unit 4, Level 4........ou, ough, augh, au /ŏ/....p. 12 |
| 71............Unit 5, Level 3........o, u, oo, ou /ŭ/...............p. 15 |
| 72............Unit 6, Level 3........ai, ay /ā/.........................p. 18 |
| 73............Unit 6, Level 4........ey, ea, ei, eigh, aigh /ā/...p. 19 |
| 74............Unit 55, Level 1........Homophones.................p. 126 |
| 75............Unit 55, Level 2........Homophones.................p. 127 |
| 76............Unit 7, Level 4........ie, ei /ē/..........................p. 23 |
| 77............Unit 7, Level 5........ei, eo, i /ē/.......................p. 24 |
| 78............Unit 14, Level 2......./wh/...............................p. 40 |
| 79............Unit 18, Level 3........ow, ou, ough /ow/..........p. 52 |
| 80............Unit 21, Level 4........er, ear, ur, our /er/..........p. 60 |
| 81............Unit 21, Level 5........ir, er, yr, ar /er/...............p. 61 |
| 82............Unit 22, Level 3........ar, aur /ar/......................p. 64 |
| 83............Unit 23, Level 2........ear, aur, are, air, ar /air/..p. 66 |
| 84............Unit 25, Level 4........or, ore /or/......................p. 72 |
| 85............Unit 26, Level 3........c(e), c(y) /s/, dge /j/.......p. 75 |
| 86............Unit 26, Level 4........ce /s/, g(i), ge, g(y) /j/....p. 76 |
| 87............Unit 29, Level 1........ff /f/...............................p. 81 |
| 88............Unit 30................g, gg, gh /g/.................p. 84 |
| 89............Unit 32, Level 3........el, il /l/............................p. 89 |
| 90............Unit 32, Level 4........al, le /l/...........................p. 90 |
| 91............Unit 33................mn, mb /m/..................p. 91 |
| 92............Unit 34................kn, gn, pn /n/...............p. 92 |
| 93............Unit 37, Level 1........ed, tt, t /t/........................p. 98 |
| 94............Unit 38................ss, z, se, s /z/..............p. 100 |

Continued from page vii

95...........Unit 39, Level 1......ough /off/, /oh/, /uf/....................................p. 101

96...........Unit 39, Level 2......ough /oo/, /ow/, /ŏ/ ....p. 102

97...........Unit 40, Level 3......ed /d/, /ed/ ....p. 105

98...........Unit 41, Level 2......--ies   --s ....p. 107

99...........Unit 42...................Add n   Add en ....p. 109

100.........Unit 43...................ish, ist, ize ....p. 110

101.........Unit 46...................sure /zhur/, ture /cher/................................p. 114

102.........Unit 47...................cia, tia /shu/, sia /zhu/ ....p. 115

103.........Unit 55, Level 3......Homophones...p. 128

104.........Unit 3, Level 3........i, y, ai, ui /ĭ/..p. 8

105.........Unit 11, Level 2......s, ch, ss, ci, ce, sh /sh/..............................p. 34

106.........Unit 15, Level 4......u-e, oo, u, ough, ou /oo/ ....p. 44

107.........Unit 17, Level 3......oi, oy /oy/..p. 49

108.........Unit 27, Level 3......Double consonants ....p. 79

109.........Unit 29, Level 3......ph, gh /f/...p. 83

110.........Unit 35, Level 2......rh, wr /r/..p. 94

111.........Unit 35, Level 3......rh, wr /r/..p. 95

112.........Unit 36, Level 1......st, sc /s/...p. 96

113.........Unit 36, Level 2......c, ce, cy /s/ ....p. 97

114.........Unit 37, Level 2......bt, pt /t/ ....p. 99

115.........Unit 41, Level 3......__o --> es   s ....p. 108

116.........Unit 44...................or, er...p. 111

117.........Unit 45, Level 1......--ion and --ian ....p. 112

118.........Unit 45, Level 2......-sion /zhun/ -tion, -sion, -cian /shun/ ....p. 113

119.........Unit 48...................--ment, --ate, --ness...................................p. 116

120.........Unit 49, Level 1......--ant ....p. 117

121.........Unit 49, Level 2......--ent, --eer ....p. 118

122.........Unit 50, Level 1......--ity, --ty ....p. 119

123.........Unit 50, Level 2......--ary ....p. 120

124.........Unit 51...................--ally, --ly, --ward ....p. 121

125.........Unit 52...................--ous /us/..p. 122

126.........Unit 53...................--cious, tious, scious /shus/; xious /kshus/ ....p. 123

127.........Unit 54, Level 1......ious /eeus/, /shus/ ....p. 124

128.........Unit 54, Level 2- ....-eous /ē-ŭs/...p. 125

FUNDAMENTALS

As you progress through the units, there are some fundamental practices that will help as you guide your students toward a better understanding of how words are constructed. The bulk of your preparation for teaching will happen in this preliminary stage of incorporating these elements into your practice.

Teach words as sounds, not series of letters. It is essential for many learners that we focus on the sounds that make words rather than spelling words by calling out the letter names. For example, when discussing the word "father," you will not spell the word ("eff, aye, tee, aich, ee, are") but you will speak the four sounds in the word: "ff, ahh, th, er." There are six letters but only four sounds. Visual learners need to learn to focus on the sequence of <u>sounds</u> they can hear in words.

Teach one sound at a time. There are a finite number of sounds in our language and these can be mastered and then used to make an infinite number of words.

Teach all the ways to spell a sound at one time. These various sound spellings are presented together so students will see how many ways there are to spell each sound. This practice eliminates a lot of confusion for the students when presented with unknown words.

For example, "short o" as in "pot" or "octopus" actually can be spelled six ways:
- o as in pot
- au as in author, august, because
- aw as in saw, awesome, lawn
- augh as in daughter, caught, naughty
- ough as in ought, brought, bought, fought, thought
- a as in father, want, water

Conversely, a cluster of letters may represent several sounds:
- ough says o as in fought
- ough says oh as in though
- ough says ow as in bough, drought, slough
- ough says uf as in rough, tough, enough,
- ough say ooo as in through
- ough says off as in cough

Color-code the target sound in each lesson. Color-coding is a powerful visual tool that helps many struggling students recognize the sound pattern in all the related words. For instance, in the "aw" lesson, the students will highlight in yellow that spelling in all the words: "fawn, lawn, dawn, yawn, law, draw, straw, crawl." All that is needed is a highlighter or yellow crayon and thirty seconds the first time the lesson is introduced. Explain that when they read the AW words, everything that is yellow says "AW."

Practice daily with whiteboard and marker. Teachers gain instant feedback on each student's understanding of the lesson, while children become active participants and are compelled to learn "from the brain out" rather than being passive listeners with marginal learning benefits. Children are given the opportunity to learn the structure of words using all their modalities. They hear the word, orally break it into sounds, and then they repeat the sounds as they represent those sounds with letters on their whiteboards. They are hearing, speaking, moving, and seeing the lesson. About fifteen minutes each day of whiteboard practice is essential for mastery of these lessons. *See "helpful hints" at the end of this section.

Group words with same sound spelling in sentences. This practice provides a framework that helps a child easily remember which words contain a particular sound spelling. Because sentences are illustrated with cartoons, the child's learning is nearly instant. The brain can record and recall a picture far more easily than a memorized sequence of letters. The sentences also enhance the students' understanding of the meaning of each word. The story bytes and cartoons engage students in their learning.

Use fingermapping as a framework for sound sequence. Fingermapping is an exciting and very effective practice that helps beginners or visual learners see a map of the the sequence of the sounds they are hearing. Many new and struggling readers reverse, insert, or omit sounds. Fingermapping prevents all this by providing students with a visual map or structure for each word. There are many students who simply cannot correctly write new words until they see the fingermap. One look at the map, and they can correctly sound and write the word. Over time, the reliance on a visual fingermap diminishes totally, but in the beginning, for some children, the visual structure is the only means by which they correctly sequence sounds and letters.

A recurring comment made by teachers first introduced to fingermapping is "Oh, I could never learn how to do that!" But like any new skill we learn, the practice of fingermapping, while it is strange in the beginning, will become automatic and easy to use. The value to students who need it far outweighs the difficulties to us. A detailed explanation of fingermapping follows.

*Helpful hints:

You do not have to purchase costly white boards from a teaching supply store. If you buy one 4'x8' shower board from a building supply store, you can have them cut the board into pieces that are 12" tall and 16" wide. One shower board will make 24 boards. You will have to purchase markers, but you can buy bundles of cheap, white tube socks to use for erasers. The children keep their markers inside the tube socks for storing in their desks, and during the lesson, the tube socks are wonderful erasers. I take them home periodically and wash them in a bleach solution.

Guidelines I set in place from the beginning include no doodling with markers during whiteboard time. Every child I have met loves markers on whiteboards and they often will become distracted by drawing lines and grids or decorating their words with flowery sorts of lines. While I am all for illustration for deepening learning, I discourage this practice during our whiteboard lesson because the children are better able to stay focused on the lesson.

FINGERMAPPING

Fingermapping is a practice I developed as I worked with Title 1 students in grades K through 7 in reading. It emerged out of repeated attempts to find something visual and concrete that would help my students grasp the structure and order of sound spellings. Fingermapping provides a visual map of words just like a map provides a visual for oral directions.

The teacher does the fingermapping as she introduces each word to her students, then repeats it while students sound the word with her. My suggestion is that at least in the beginning, a teacher practice finger mapping each list of words before presenting the lesson. Over time, the action of fingermapping will become automatic.

1. Basics of Fingermapping

For words containing up to five letters, the teacher will use the left hand, held up with palm facing the students (*figure 1*):

Figure 1

From this point on, thumb is finger #1, pointer is finger #2, "tall man" is finger #3, ring is finger #4, and pinkie is finger #5. Each finger represents one letter. The illustrations in this section will show what you see as you are finger mapping. Note that the words will appear backwards to you.

In a word such as "cat," there are three letters and three distinct sounds: "c – a – t" so the map would look like this (see *figure 2*). The only time fingers are displayed touching each other is when two or more letters represent one sound ("igh" in night or "ai" in rain).

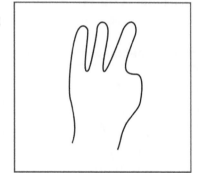

Figure 2

When you present the lesson for the first time, follow this sequence:

1. Say, "When I say, 'Ready,' that is your signal that we are going to start a new word. You will look at me, listen as I say the word, then listen as I sound it. Let me model for you."

2. Say, "Cat." Cat has three letters (hold up your three fingers as in figure 2) and three sounds." Point to the tip of your tall man finger as you sound C (not letter name). Point to the tip of your ring finger as you sound A, and to the tip of your pinkie finger as you sound T.

3. "Now you sound out "cat" with me." Repeat sounding as you point to each finger tip with students joining you. Remember, you are mapping backwards to YOU so that the word map will appear correct to the students (*figure 3*).

4. Say, "Now sound out 'cat' again, but this time, write the sounds as you say them on your whiteboard. When you say 'c,' write it, when you say 'a,' write it, and when you say 't' write it." Be sure you do not say letter names, but rather sounds: 'c' as in cave, 'a' as in ant, and 't' as in top. Some students will readily sound and write, while others will appear determined to NOT sound. It is critical for all students to sound as they write, so they will all place the correct sounds in the right sequence.

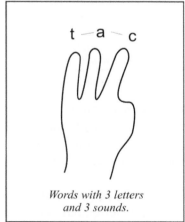

Words with 3 letters and 3 sounds.

Figure 3

5. Do a quick visual check of whiteboards and then say, "Ready" and repeat the steps with the next word.

In time, this process should evolve into crisp, one-word directions:
- Say, "Ready?"
- Say, "The word is, 'sand.'"
- Say, "/s/ /a/ /n/ /d/."
- Say, "Sound it with me."
- All together say, "/s/ /a/ /n/ /d/."
- Say, "Sound and write." (Students will sound and write on whiteboards.)
- Do a rapid visual check.
- Correct if needed by fingermapping and identifying the sound for each finger or finger cluster.
- Repeat process for next word.

Do all within your power to break students of the habit of looking at the printed word and then copying it to their whiteboards. If children rely on copying words they see, they will miss the power of hearing and representing sounds. Insist that all of them can hear the sounds and write what they hear. If you notice that there are problems with representing the words with letters (whether omissions, reversals, or additions) show them the fingermap again.

2. Fingermapping Blends

Remember that each finger represents a letter. When finger mapping "flag" or "stop" you will use four fingers, # 2-5, each separate from the other (*figure 4*). Blends such as "fl" or "st" are two distinct sounds, not one. Blends do not need to be taught separately because children can distinctly hear the sounds of each letter in the blend. Not so with digraphs (sh) or diphthongs (oi) which are combinations of letters that form a new sound together.

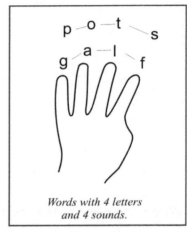

Words with 4 letters and 4 sounds.

Figure 4

When finger mapping and sounding "flag," hold up four fingers, and while pointing to each fingertip, say four separate sounds: /f/, /l/, /a/, /g/. The map will be the same for any other four letter word with four distinct, separate sounds: stop, sand, stem, pant, bent, tent, etc.

Words with 5 letters and 5 sounds.

Figure 5

Words such as "stand," "plant," and "frank" require five fingers, each separate from the other (*figure 5*). Again, in those words, despite initial and final consonant blends, each sound may be heard distinctly, so each sound requires one finger in mapping.

3. Fingermapping Sounds With Multiple Letters

Vowel teams require more than one letter to produce. For example, in "play" it takes both a and y to make the long a sound. In "rain" the combination of a and i produces the sound of long a. In "road and read," the vowel teams of oa and ea produce one distinct sound together.

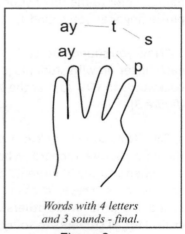

Words with 4 letters and 3 sounds - final.

Figure 6

At this point, you will need to explain to the children that each finger represents one written letter, but because some sounds require more than one letter, those fingers in the map will be bundled close together.

In *figure 6*, you will find the map for any four letter word ending in a vowel team.

If the vowel team is found inside the word (such as rain or goat), the finger map would vary slightly as shown in *figure 7*.

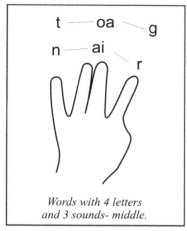

Words with 4 letters and 3 sounds- middle.

Figure 7

4. Digraphs are taught similarly to how we teach vowel teams. Tell the students that sometimes letters forget their normal sounds when they get near other letters and then together the letters form a totally different sound.

For instance, display the letters S, T, H, C, W, and P. You can show the children that when you put /h/ next to/s/, the letters do not say /s/ /h/ anymore, but rather they lose their heads and say /sh/ when together. The same goes for putting /h/ next to any of the remaining displayed letters!

Drive this lesson home by assigning a sound to each student. One is S, one T, one H, etc. I then have them role play how sounds combine and "get silly" and forget the sounds they are supposed to make. First I have S walk back and forth saying her sound "ssss". Then I have H join her and as they go back and forth, they now say "shhh". I repeat this with the other letters: T and H saying TH as in "thin", C and H saying CH as in "chip", W and H saying WH as in "what", and finally P and H saying fff as in "phone."

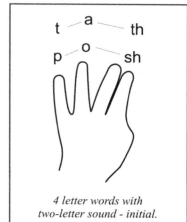

4 letter words with two-letter sound - initial.

Figure 8

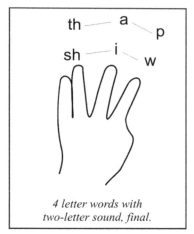

4 letter words with two-letter sound, final.

Figure 9

5. Diphthongs are presented the same way. These include "ou" "oi" "ow" "oy".

Figures 8 and following illustrate finger mapping for various types of words:

• <u>Initial digraph or diphthong</u> – *figure 8*. Examples of words include "**sh**ip, **sh**op, **th**at, **ch**op, **ch**ip, **ou**rs," and any other four letter words with an initial two letter sound.

• <u>Final digraph or diphthong</u> – *figure 9*. Examples of words would include "wi**sh**, di**sh**, ca**sh**, la**sh**, s**low**, st**ew**, pa**th**," and any other word with a final two letter sound.

• <u>Middle digraph or diphthong</u> – *figure 10*. Examples of words are myriad: "br**ow**n, cl**ow**n, cl**ou**d, st**ou**t," etc.

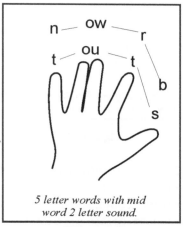

5 letter words with mid word 2 letter sound.

Figure 10

6. Fingermapping Letter Clusters

Wherever the letter cluster appears in the word, that is where the fingers will also cluster that represent each sound.

For example:
• eigh-t   (2 sounds, 5 letters), first 4 fingers together, 5th finger separate.
• sh-ou-t   (3 sounds, five letters), fingers 1-2 and 3-4 grouped, 5th finger separate.
• r-u-nn-er   (4 sounds, 6 letters), fingers 1 and 2 separate, 3-4 together and 5-6 together.
• f-a-th-er   (4 sounds, six letters), see figure 11.
• t-augh-t   (3 sounds, 6 letters), and so on. First finger separate, fingers 2-5 together, thumb of other hand for final t.

When you need more than five fingers to spell a word, simply bring fingers from your right hand, starting with finger #1, which is your thumb. See example for "father" in *figure 11*.

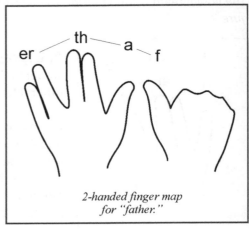

2-handed finger map for "father."

Figure 11

Specific fingermapping guidelines will be presented in each lesson if any tricky situation should present itself.

The question has been asked whether or not the students should finger map. I have never asked the children to finger map because the power for them in fingermapping is totally visual. To ask them to finger map will simply present them with an unnecessary skill to learn at a time when the simpler a lesson can be for them, the better!

7. Fingermapping Silent E

Fingermapping Pinchy E: long vowel and silent final E.

Figure 12

Silent E can be very tricky for students who struggle with reading. We teach children to sound out words and they grind to a halt in the face of undecodable sound spellings and "silent" letters. In the case of the final, silent E, explain that the E is teaming up with other letters. In the case of long vowel spellings, the E is silent, but busy pinching the preceding vowel.

Notice in figure 12 that the example word "tame" has four letters, but we can only hear three. 4 letters = 4 fingers. But the E at the end makes no sound. He is busy pinching the A to make it say its name.

Examples of words with final, silent pinchy E:
• tame, lame, came, game, ate, etc., page 16
• Eve, Pete, these page 20
• five, live, white, mice, while, etc. page 26

Examples of words with final silent E when NOT pinchy E: (fig. 13)
• live, give page 7
• some, come, shove, above, dove, love page 14
• please, grease page 22. E is not pinching. The vowels are long vowel teams.
• whittle, whistle page 40
• gaggle, wiggle, struggle page 84
• simple, little, purple, people, sample, maple, apple page 88
• whistle, bustle, rustle, castle page 96
• pause, browse, lose, tease, cruise, freeze, snooze page 100

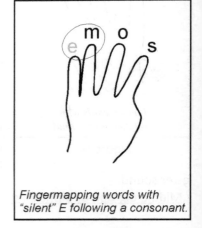

Fingermapping words with "silent" E following a consonant.

Figure 13

8. Fingermapping Multiple Syllable Words

When you get to **very long words**, what works best is to fingermap each syllable separately.
Example: neigh-bor-hood, ad-ven-ture, fur-ni-ture, de-men-tia, par-ti-ci-pant, em-ploy, ment, un-for-tu-nate. This way you don't run out of fingers and the children can see that big words can be easily broken into manageable chunks. Have children separate words into syllables by drawing slash marks between them.

Fingermapping ING show three fingers together to represent that word chunk either as one syllable (r-ing) or as a multi-syllable word (tap-ing). In this book the sound spelling is actually NG to accommodate all spellings: ang, ing, ung, ong, etc.

For compound words, fingermap each word separately. Example: under-stood.
Or better yet, you can map by syllables: un-der-stood.

DAILY ROUTINE

Preparation

Make enough copies of the lesson to give each child his or her own copy - and one for teacher.
Give each child a yellow highlighter or crayon to use for coloring the sound spelling.
Each child will also need a whiteboard and dry erase marker.

Day 1

• Pass out the lesson and highlighter.
• Identify the target sound spelling.
• Have children color only those letters which combine to make the target sound.
• Draw attention to the fact that the letters that are left not colored can easily be sounded out.
• Using whiteboards and markers, play Quick Draw. If you have a classroom whiteboard, let the kids stand at the board. Otherwise, they can use individual whiteboards.

HOW TO PLAY QUICK DRAW:
• Say the first word while the children listen.
• Hold up fingers to show the structure of the word. One finger for each letter. If two or more letters combine to make a sound, those fingers will be close together. (Refer to instructions for fingermapping).
• As you point to each finger, sound out the word, making sure the children are watching and sounding with you.
• Say, "Sound and write." The children need to each say the sounds in the word as they write. Many will try to just go straight to writing, but it is important for them to orally sound, as this will guide them into correctly writing the word. If your child struggles with writing, let him or her use pull-down letters to form the words.
• Do a quick visual check for errors. If there is a mistake, do the fingermapping again, asking the child to sound with you to find out where the error is.

Day 2

• Ask the children to tell you the target sound spelling.
• Review the sentences containing their words.
• Play Quick Draw with the words. You may include other words with the same sound spelling as you feel the children are comfortable.

Day 3

• Review the sound spellings quickly.
• Review the sentences.
• Do a pretest with the words in order to find out where trouble spots might be.
• Use fingermapping as needed.

Day 4

• Play Quick Draw, and this time include other words that follow the sound spelling in the lesson.
• If the children are ready, go ahead and do the assessment.
• Give the children the opportunity to review and retake if they don't make 100%. As time goes by, you will find the children will learn their list of words very quickly and you might be able to go to only 3 sessions a week.

Sound Spellings and Their Key Words*

Short Vowels:

a	at
au	laugh

e	red
ea	head
ai	said
ie	friend

i	it
y	myth
ai	certain
ui	build

o	on
a	want
aw	saw
au	haul
al	walk
ou	cough
ough	bought
augh	caught

u	up
o	mother
ou	rough
o--e	come
oe	does
oo	flood

Sounds of Y

y	my
y	funny
y	myth

Diphthongs:

oi	join
oy	joy

ou	out
ow	cow
ough	drought

Sounds of 'ough'

ough	though
ough	tough
ough	through
ough	thought
ough	bough
ough	cough

Long Vowels:

a--e	ate
ai	rain
ay	day
ey	they
ea	break
eigh	eight
ei	rein
aigh	straight

e	he
ea	eat
eo	people
e--e	Pete
ey	key
ee	see
ie	chief
i--e	petite
i	Maria
ei	ceiling
y	funny

i	find
ie	pie
i--e	like
igh	high
eigh	height
y	my
eye	eye
is	isle
ais	aisle

o	go
ow	snow
oa	goat
o--e	home
oe	Joe
ough	though
oo	poor
ou	your

u--e	use
ue	cue
u	pupil
ew	few

Long 'OO'

oo	cool
ew	new
o-e	lose
u-e	flute
ue	blue
ui	suit
ou	you
oe	shoe
o	to
ough	through
u	flu

Short 'OO'

oo	book
oul	could
u	put

Bossy R
/er/

ur	turn
ir	girl
or	worm
er	her
ear	learn
yr	syrup
ar	dollar
our	tourist

/ar/

ar	star
ear	heart
uar	guard

/or/

or	for
ore	more
ar	warm
our	your
oor	door

/air/

ar	vary
air	pair
ear	pear
are	care
ere	where
eir	their
uar	guarantee

/ear/

eer	deer
ier	pier
ere	here
ear	near

Digraphs

sh	she
s	sure
ch	machine
ss	assure
ci	special
ce	ocean

ch	child
tch	catch

th	the
th	with

wh	when

zh

s	measure
si	television

/ng/ /ngk/

nk	wink
ng	king

/F/ Spellings

f	fun
ph	phone
gh	tough
ff	off

/G/ Spellings

g	got
gh	ghost
gg	baggy

/H/ Spellings

h	hot
wh	who

/J/ Spellings

j	jam
ge	large, gel
dge	fudge
g(y)	gym
g(i)	giant

/K/ /KW/ Spellings

k	kiss
c	cat
ck	kick
ch	Chris
qu	queen

/L/ Spellings

l	left
ll	well
el	parcel
le	little
il	fossil
al	rural

/M/ Spellings

m	my
mm	summer
mb	lamb
mn	autumn

/N/ Spellings

n	not
nn	dinner
kn	know
gn	gnat
pn	pneumonia

/R/ Spellings

r	ran
rr	arrow
wr	wren
rh	rhino
re	here

/S/ Spellings

s	sit
ss	glass
c(e)	cent
st	whistle
sc	scent
se	horse
ce	lace
c(y)	cyclops
c(i)	city

/T/ Spellings

t	tap
tt	matter
bt	doubt
pt	pterodactyl
ed	passed

/Z/ Spellings

z	zoo
zz	fizz
s	his
se	lose
ze	snooze
x	xylophone

*W, V, P, B, D not included because the sounds of these consonants are not made with other letters.

USING KEYWORDS EFFECTIVELY

If you refer to the chart on the previous page, "Sound Spellings and Their Keywords," you'll find that we have identified and grouped the sound spellings together and that each sound spelling has a related keyword. For example, in the box for the sound oo, there are three sound spellings: OO as in "book," OUL as in "could," and U as in "put."

We chose the smallest words we could for keywords in order to accommodate beginners; however, having identified a keyword, it will be simple to gather far more complex words around each keyword.

In my kindergarten classroom, each time we learned a sound spelling, we'd write the keyword at the top of a long strip of paper, then post it on the wall. As children came across words containing that sound spelling, they wrote them on the strip. In a kindergarten classroom, the list of words might look like this at first: "star," "far," "car," "part," "art," "tar." Then over time, words can be added: "smart," "park," "start," "party," "depart," "department," and so on.

If you are working with older students, you can use keywords to help them analyze longer words.

You teach sounds and their spellings,

Sound:	Sound:
/er/	/oo/
Sound Spellings:	Sound Spellings:
er, ir, or, ur, ear, yr, ar, our	oo, oul, u
Keywords:	Keywords:
her, girl, worm, turn, learn	book, could, put
syrup, dollar, tourist.	

the child encounters a new word,

understood

and uses known words to analyze it.

her   book

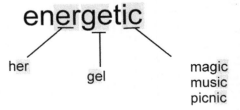

Even in a long word, once sound spellings are highlighted,
what is left are letters that are easy to decode.

neighborhood

eight   worm   book

The more you focus on sound spellings and analyzing new words with your students, the more fluent your students will become at identifying those spelling patterns and using them to figure out new words. This practice is especially valuable for all those dominant right-brained learners!

Sounds Spelling Tracking Sheet

Write your students' names on the lines provided. Check off each sound mastered in the boxes which are numbered by unit.

Name	1	2	3	4	5	6	7	8	9	10	11	12	13	14	15	16	17	18	19	20	21	22	23	24	25	26	27	28

Child1st Publications LLC | child1st.com | 800-881-0912

Sounds Spelling Tracking Sheet, continued

Write your students' names on the lines provided. Check off each sound mastered in the boxes which are numbered by unit.

Name	29	30	31	32	33	34	35	36	37	38	39	40	41	42	43	44	45	46	47	48	49	50	51	52	53	54	55

Child1st Publications LLC | child1st.com | 800-881-0912

TEACHING NOTES

Follow Lesson Sequence pgs. xi-xii. Use Teaching Notes to prepare teacher's copy before teaching lesson.
At the beginning of each lesson, students will highlight target sounds.

#	UNIT/LEVEL	CONTENT	PAGE	NOTES - see also fingermapping notes at the bottom of the page on each lesson.
1	1-1	Short A	1	Page xi, Section 1. All words are made of single letter sounds which are easily heard. Follow the Lesson Sequence for every lesson. See pages xi-xii.
2	2-1	Short E	3	All words are made of single letter sounds. Say each sound and write a letter as you say each sound.
3	3-1	Short I	6	All words are made of single letter sounds. See notes Lesson 1.
4	4-1	Short O	9	Single letter sounds except "OFF." Underline FF. 2 letters, 1 sound. From now on, each time you find a sound needs more than one letter, underline them on your sheet.
5	5-1	Short U	13	All words are made of single letter sounds. Sound and write all individual sounds.
6	1-2	Short A	2	Single letter sounds except for "L AU GH." AU=short A. GH=/F/. Underline AU and GH. This will be covered again on page 82.
7	11-1	/SH/ (Sounds like SH)	33	Highlight all SH and CE (in OCEAN). From now on, underline all multiple letter sounds.
8	12-1	/TH/ (Sounds like TH)	35	Highlight TH's. Highlight multiple letter sounds such as EY in THEY.
9	13-1	/CH/ (Sounds like CH)	37	Highlight CH. Underline EA in EACH, OW in CHOW, LL in CHILL. 2 letters, one sound. Note that EACH has only two sounds: E and CH. CHOW also just has two sounds: CH and OW.
10	2-2	Short E	4	All words are made of single letter sounds except for LL in 4 words. Underline LL.
11	3-2	Short I	7	Underline 2 letter sounds: LL, TH, SH, CK, VE (see pg. xiv Fig 13 for "silent" final E).
12	19-1	NG and NK	53	Highlight target sounds: NG and NK. Sound and write all other (individual) sounds.
13	4-2	Short O	10	Underline SS, NG, AL, CH. All other sounds are 1-letter sounds. See note on lesson re AL.
14	6-1	Long A	16	See page xiv Fig 12. Pinchy E is silent but pinches the vowel to make it long. So he has a finger when mapping the word, but his lips are pinched shut. Draw a little curve under the word from Pinchy E to the vowel he is pinching to show they are connected.
15	6-2	Long A	17	Underline TH. Highlight target spellings. All other sounds are 1-letter sounds.
16	7-1	Long E	20	See page xiv Fig 12. Pinchy E for EVEN, EVE, PETE, THESE. Draw curves for Pinchy E to vowels he is pinching. Underline TH.
17	20-1	Sounds of Y	55	Underline double letters and CH. Sound and write all other individual sounds.
18	8-1	Long I	25	Underline CH, WH. Sound and write all other individual sounds.
19	8-2	Long I	26	Pinchy E rule, pg. xiv, Fig 12. Draw curves for Pinchy E. Underline WH and IE which are 1 sound but 2 letters.
20	8-3	Long I	27	Highlight target spellings (IGH, EIGH, IS, AIS, EYE). Sounds require 3-4 letters/fingers.
21	32-1	/L/ (Sounds like L)	87	Underline IE in LIE. PUPIL is only IL word: (where IL sounds like L).
22	9-1	Long O	28	Underline TH. All other words are made of single letter sounds.
23	9-2	Long O	29	Curve for Pinchy E. Note: in blends such as STR, all sounds are heard so have the students say each sound as they are sounding and writing. There is no benefit in teaching blends as it just makes more for children to memorize - something visual learners don't do well.
24	9-3	Long O	30	Underline SH, KN, TH. Highlight target sounds which are 2-letter sounds.
25	10	Long U	32	Highlight. Underline IL in PUPIL. UNITE, USE, FUSE, MULE are Pinchy E words. Draw curves for them.
26	15-1	/OO/ "cool"	41	Underline WH in WHOM /H/. Underline AY, TH, ER. SUPER, FLUTE are Pinchy E words.
27	15-2	/OO/	42	Underline TH, SH, LL, WH (/H/), ED in MOVED /D/.
28	16-1	/OO/	45	Underline LL, SH.
29	17-1	/OY/	47	Highlight the target sounds from the top of the page. There are no multiple letter sounds to underline.
30	18-1	/OW/	50	Underline SE in HOUSE. See page xiv Fig 13.
31	21-1	/ER/	57	Underline ERE in WERE and VE in SERVE.

#	UNIT/LEVEL	CONTENT	PAGE	NOTES - see also fingermapping notes at the bottom of the page on each lesson.
32	21-2	/ER/	58	Underline TH, SH, CH, NG
33	22-1	/AR/	62	No special notes. Follow lesson sequence.
34	22-2	/AR/	63	Underline GE in LARGE and CHARGE, CH. Slash to separate syllables in MARKET, SCARLET.
35	31-1	/K/	85	Underline LE in TAC<u>LE</u>, SS in KI<u>SS</u>. Pinchy E words: PIKE, BIKE, CAKE, CAVE.
36	31-2	/K/ and /QU/	86	Underline EE, AR, ZE, OO. QU starts out sounding like K, but ends up sounding like KW.
37	2-3	Short E	5	Slashes between syllables - map syllables separately. Page xiv Section 8.
38	4-3	Short O	11	Underline TH, ER, WH, TCH, SH.
39	5-2	Short U	14	Underline ER, TH and consonant+E pairs at bottom of page. See Fig. 13 page xiv.
40	23-1	/AIR/ R Controlled	65	Underline WH, TH, CH. See hint for THEIR at bottom of lesson.
41	24-1	/EAR/ R Controlled	67	Underline SH, CH
42	24-2	/EAR/ R Controlled	68	Underline ED in PIER<u>CED</u> where ED /T/.
43	25-1	/OR/ R Controlled	69	Underline OI and SE separately in TORTOISE. OI /i/ and SE /S/.
44	25-2	/OR/	70	Underline CH, ER, TH, NG. You may separate HORNET, FORGET, and MORNING into syllables and map each syllable separately.
45	26-1	/S/ and /J/	73	In column 1, CE is a sound spelling that sounds like S, but the E also is a Pinchy E reaching back to the A to make it say its name. In column 2, G sounds like J when followed by E, I and Y at the beginnings of words, but also GE sounds like J when at the end of a word such as LAR<u>GE</u>. Underline LE, IE, LL, FFE.
46	26-2	C /S/ and G /J/	74	In column 1, CE sounds like S at the ends of words. Those endings will require 2 letters to spell the S sound. In the words where C is followed by an I, only the C will be highlighted as the I's that follow either are R Controlled (IR) or they make their own sound (ex: CITY) In column 2, GE and DGE sound like a J.
47	27-1	Double Consonant	77	Underline double consonants and ER. Students can make a slash mark between syllables, dividing each word between matching consonants.
48	27-2	Double Consonant	78	Underline double consonants, ED /D/ in columns 1-2, ED /T/ at the bottom, WR, and NG.
49	7-2	Long E	21	Underline SH, WH, CH, SE (in CHEESE), NN in FUNNY.
50	7-3	Long E	22	Underline SE in PLEASE and GREASE, LL in REALLY, VE in LEAVE, and WH in WHEAT.
51	9-4	Long O	31	Underline TH. See also page 71 for OU spelling that is R Controlled as in YOUR.
52	12-2	TH	36	Draw curves for Pinchy E words. Underline EE, TH, ER, CK, NK, EI, ERE. Note that TOGETHER is easy to learn to spell if you separate into 3 parts: TO-GET-HER. "We will get her together."
53	13-2	/CH/	38	Underline TH in THATCH.
54	14-1	WH	39	Underline ERE, CH, EE, and ED /D/. Curve for Pinchy E in WHALE.
55	15-3	/OO/ "cool"	43	Underline SE in BRUISE, TH in THROUGH.
56	16-2	/OO/	46	Underline SH, SS, ED /T/ in LOOKED. Slashes for syllables.
57	17-2	/OY/	48	Underline SE in NOISE, CE in VOICE, ER.
58	18-2	/OW/	51	Underline ER, TH, SH, SE in MOUSE, Pinchy E in OUTSIDE. Slash syllables.
59	28	Schwa /UH/	80	Underline vowel teams EE, OU, AI, AY, EA, and VE ending in ABOVE. 3 Pinchy E curves.
60	19-2	NG and /NGK/	54	Underline OR and TH.
61	20-2	Y /Long E/	56	Underline double consonants, ER, CH, CK, and QU.
62	21-3	/ER/	59	Underline EY in TURKEY, AR in ARMOR, SE in WORSE, and TH.
63	25-3	/OR/	71	Underline TH, SE, GE. Teach "OUR" words depending on your pronunciation of TOURIST.
64	29-2	/F/	82	Three Pinchy E words in column 1. Underline OU and AU spellings in column 2.
65	32-2	/L/	88	Draw slashes to separate syllables in long words. Underline double consonants. Under-line R Controlled pairs: UR, ER, OR. EO, OY.
66	35-1	/R/	93	Draw slashes to separate syllables. Underline TH, ME in RHYME, and NG in WRONG. 3 Pinchy E words RHODE, WRITE, WROTE. Draw curves for Pinchy E.
67	40-1	Past Tense	103	Underline double consonants. Underline AY and AR, EE, AI in column 2. You can hear both sounds in the -ED ending starting with WANTED and ending with WAITED. 2 sounds = 2 fingers when fingermapping.

#	UNIT/LEVEL	CONTENT	PAGE	NOTES - see also fingermapping notes at the bottom of the page on each lesson.
68	40-2	Past Tense	104	Underline double consonants and CK, CH, WR, EA, OR, OW, OA. From HEADED to TREATED, you can hear both sounds in the final -ED. Two sounds and two fingers.
69	41-1	Plurals S and ES	106	Underline double consonants, R Controlled (IR, ER, AR), Diphthong OY, and vowel teams EA, OA. Underline CK. Digraph SH. The sound of S in the first column is like Z. In the second column, you can hear both sounds in the final -ES. Two sounds=two fingers.
70	4-4	Short O	12	Underline TH, GH /F/ in COUGH, MN /M/ in AUTUMN, ER, SE in BECAUSE.
71	5-3	Short U	15	Underline GH /F/, CH, NG, and ER. Use slashes to separate syllables.
72	6-3	Long A	18	Slash syllables. Underline SH, FF, CH. Note: AY spelling is mostly found at the end of a word or a syllable. Ex: AWAY is at end of word while PAY|MENT has AY at end of syllable.
73	6-4	Long A	19	Underline OR and GN in REIGN.
74	55-1	Homophones	126	Underline vowel teams AY, EIGH, EA, AI and draw curves for Pinchy E spellings. Underline LL in SELL and CELL.
75	55-2	Homophones	127	Underline R Controlled spellings: ERE, EAR, ERE, EIR. Underline KN, OU, SC.
76	7-4	Long E	23	Underline TH, CH, SH, NG. Underline consonant+E endings -CE, -VE, -ZE, -NE.
77	7-5	Long E	24	Underline ZE in SEIZE and -SURE (see page 114). For EIR in WEIRD, see also the R Controlled spelling lesson on page 68. Underline NG, -VE, -PT, -TE, -LE.
78	14-2	WH	40	Underline ER, OO, LE, CK, IR, SH. Draw curves for Pinchy E words: WHILE, WHITE.
79	18-3	/OW/	52	Draw slashes for syllables. Underline LL, TH, AI, ER, -CE endings, CH, AR.
80	21-4	/ER/	60	Underline VE, CE, SE, GE. Underline CH, TH, RR, EW, AI. Use slashes for syllables. "OUR" words included depending on your pronunciation of TOURIST. Or see page 71 for /OR/.
81	21-5	/ER/	61	Use slashes to separate words into syllables. Underline double consonants, QU, VE ending. Draw curves to show Pinchy E for PURFUME and CIRCULATE.
82	22-3	/AR/	64	Underling UE in ARGUE, LE, TH, ER, CH, NG. Note that UAR /AR/ in GUARD is a 3-letter sound spelling. Any word that has "guard" in it will share that spelling. For example, guardian, lifeguard, etc. Draw slashes to show syllables.
83	23-2	/AIR/	66	Draw slashes to separate syllables. Underline SH, EE.
84	25-4	/OR/	72	Slashes for syllables. Underline AU, TH, ERE, AR, CE, ER, OUS, RR. Curve for Pinchy E.
85	26-3	C /S/ and G /J/	75	Underline EI, AR, ER, UR. Use slashes for syllables.
86	26-4	C /S/ and G /J/	76	Underline OUR, GG & double consonants. Note that in column 1, you will highlight -CE endings and G /J/ at the beginnings of words. In column 2, highlight -GE endings.
87	29-1	/F/	81	Use slashes for syllables. Underline -ED /D/ endings, ER, OR, IR, double consonants.
88	30	/G/	84	Underline OU /OO/, TT, -ER, EE, -LE, IR, EA, OA, NG, double consonants.
89	32-3	/L/	89	Use slashes for syllables. Underline OU, AR, SS, OU.
90	32-4	/L/	90	Use slashes for syllables. Map syllables separately. Underline TION in RATIONAL - see page 113 example NATION. Underline IS /I/ and AIS /I/ and TT.
91	33	/M/	91	Underline AU, TH, ER.
92	34	/N/	92	Use slashes for syllables. Underline EW, CK, EE, CK, ER, AW, KN. Two Pinchy E words - GNOME and KNIFE.
93	37-1	/T/	98	Underline double consonants, OO, NG, -VE, -CE, ER.
94	38	/Z/	100	Slashes for syllables. Underline PH, AU, OW, EA, UI, EE, OO, SS, OR. Pinchy E on XYLOPHONE, PHASE, ARISE, AMAZE.
95	39-1	Sounds of OUGH	101	Fingermapping for first column is C-OU-GH, T-R-OU-GH, R-OU-GH, T-OU-GH, E-N-OU-GH, S-L-OU-GH. Second column: TH-OUGH. A-L-TH-OUGH. Underline OU, GH, OUGH, TH.
96	39-2	Sounds of OUGH	102	Underline TH. In this lesson, the OUGH is mapped as one sound in all the words. TH-R-OUGH, B-OUGH, S-L-OUGH, etc.
97	40-3	Past Tense	105	Separate syllables with slashes. Underline sounds with multiple letters such as AI, ER and double consonants. In column 1, ED has one sound /D/. In column 2, there are two distinct sounds: E and D. Underline OR, OI, ER and double consonants.
98	41-2	Plurals IES, S	107	Use slashes to separate syllables. Underline AR, OR, PP, ER, EA, OU, CH, AY, IE, DG, LL, EY, OA. The -ES endings on WOLVES, LOAVES, HALVES are one sound, but two letters. The AL in HALVES is one sound unless you are used to pronouncing the L in that word.

#	UNIT/LEVEL	CONTENT	PAGE	NOTES - see also fingermapping notes at the bottom of the page on each lesson.
99	42	Ends N or EN	109	Slashes for syllables. Underline IGH, AIGH, OR and double consonants. In column 1, the root words end in an E already so you only add an N and you can hear both the E and the N in those words. In column 2, FRIGHTEN and STRAIGHTEN add an EN, but the bottom two words require the doubling of the T so the E in EN won't pinch the vowel and make it long.
100	43	Ends ISH, IST, IZE	110	Use slashes for separating syllables. Underline CH, OO, SC, AR, OUR, OR, AR, ER, SH.
101	46	/ZHUR/ /CHER/	114	Use slashes. Underline vowel teams in column 1. Apart from those, these longer words are super easy to sound and write when done a syllable at a time.
102	47	/SHUH/ /ZHUH/	115	Underline AR, OR, ER, EE. Use slashes to separate syllables.
103	55-3	Homophones	128	Use slashes. Underline all multi-letter sounds. LE, AI, EIGH, OA, SE, OUR, EI, ER.
104	3-3	Short I	8	Use slashes. Underline ER, SH, OU, TH.
105	11-2	/SH/	34	Use slashes. Underline URE, UE, ION (see page 113), AR, -NE, OR, OU, OE, OW, LL, EAR, NG. IOUS is a special ending taught on page 124.
106	15-4	/OO/	44	Slashes. Underline LE, EA, TH, -VE, -NE. Pinchy E in column 2 - mark with a curve.
107	17-3	/OY/	49	The words in this lesson are long but not hard. Use slashes to break them up first. Underline double consonants. Underline GE ending, OUS (see page 122), CE ending, ER, ED /D/, TURE (see page 114), NG.
108	27-3	Double Consonant	79	Slashes for syllables. Underline double letters. Underline IR, OR, ER, OU, AI, -LE, -CE, ED /D/, -VE, AU, AL in APPROVAL, TION. Note Pinchy E words and draw curves.
109	29-3	/F/	83	Slashes. Underline AR, EA, OE, OR, CIAN (see page 113). Pinchy E.
110	35-2	/R/	94	Use slashes for the longer words. Underline EU in RHEUMATISM /Long U/. Underline LE ending on two words, NG, NK and ER ending. In the first column, we encounter Pinchy Vowels other than E. In RHYNE and RHYZOMES, there is a Pinchy E. In RHESUS, the U is pinching the E. In RHETORIC, the I pinches the O and in RHAPSODY, the final Y acts as a vowel and pinches the O. Make sure students understand what the words mean in this lesson. RHYNE is a river, RHESUS is a monkey, RHEUMATISM is pain in joints and or muscles, while RHIZOMES are shoots sent out underground in order to form a new plant nearby. RHETORIC refers to effective persuasive speaking, RHAPSODY refers to music that expresses a lot of emotion. WRANGLE = argue, WRATH = anger.
111	35-3	/R/	95	Slashes for syllables. Underline AR in RHUBARB, IGH in WRIGHT, NG and ER in WRANGLER, CH, TCH, and CK in the next three words. AI and TH in WRAITH, ST and LE in WRESTLE, EA and TH in WREATH. A WRAITH is a ghost. Underline double consonants.
112	36-1	/S/	96	Slashes for syllables. Underline WH and LE in the first column. OR, CE, LL, AR in the second column. A BUSTLE was a poof of fabric under a skirt to make it stick out. It also means a lot of activity. Other words are defined at the bottom of the lesson.
113	36-2	/S/	97	Slashes for syllables. Highlight the target sound spellings first. Note that in GROCERY, the E performs two functions. It helps C be soft and it is also R Controlled ER. Underline ER, OR, and AR (in CYLINDAR). To CONCEAL means to hide.
114	37-2	/T/	99	Use slashes to separate syllables. Highlight target spellings. Note the word definitions at the bottom of the page. Underline LE and AI in PTOMAINE.
115	41-3	Plural Suffixes	108	In this lesson, syllables are important to identify and map separately. Also watch for little words inside larger ones. After marking the syllables, note the small words and ask the students to underline them as desired. I see QUIT and TOES in MOSQUITOES. POT and TOES in POTATOES, etc. In this column also note the headings for each group of words. In the first group, all words end in O and to make a plural you add ES. In the second group, the words end in F and to make a plural you remove the F and add VES. At the bottom, words ended in Y and you remove the Y and add IES. In column 2 at the top, the reason the first word has an S ending is because they are plural. More than one passer, more than one mother, more than one father. At the bottom of the column, we have plurals as well, but the plural refers to the whole word. Underline multiple letter sounds.
116	44	Suffixes OR, ER	111	Definitely draw slashes for syllables. Locate and underline all multi-letter sounds such as double consonants, AY, OR, ER, SH, TCH, AR. The main focus of this lesson is to identify which words end in OR and which end in ER. In this situation, the sentences that group like words together and their illustrations will provide strong memory prompts. Encourage the students to read one column and study the illustrations. They also can over-pronounce the endings OR and ER when they say the words.

#	UNIT/LEVEL	CONTENT	PAGE	NOTES - see also fingermapping notes at the bottom of the page on each lesson.
117	45-1	Suffixes ION, IAN	112	Again, slashes for syllables. Focus on the difference between ION and IAN endings. Discuss each sentence and study its illustration so the students understand what is going on in each one. The "solution" in the first sentence is to move away from the snake. Poor guy having to cry through cutting up a million onions! The librarian probably wants the custodian to stop telling jokes and start cleaning! The electrician is guarding the musician from being interrupted while practicing. Underline AR in LIBRARIAN and UAR in GUARDIAN. For ION suffix, note the "eye on" picture at left. Underline doubles.
118	45-2	Suffixes SION, TION, CIAN	113	Syllables. Highlighting. Read sentences together and discuss what each one means. In the first sentence, there was a car which crashed and then sank in the water. Students can make up what might be going on. Which election? Election about what? Is it something that is being voted on that will affect plantations? For those space fans, sentence 3 might be interesting. The visual cue for CIAN is "See I Ann" - C-I-AN. ER, LL, SS
119	48	Suffixes MENT, ATE, NESS	116	Slashes for syllables. Highlight target spellings. In this lesson MENT as a suffix means the action of (the root word). For example AMUSEMENT is the action of being amused. ARGUMENT is the action of arguing, and so on. Note how the illustrations show the meaning of the words in the sentences. For the sake of expanding vocabulary and increasing comprehension, really take time to discuss each sentence/illustration until you are sure your students get it. Underline AR, OY, GE, CC, ER, RR, SS, OR, MM, LE, CK. Now go back and draw curves under the words to show Pinchy E. (E in AMUSEMENT, ARGUMENT. The endings of the last six words in the first column and the first three in column 2.
120	49-1	Suffix ANT	117	Slashes for syllables. Again, focus on meaning and comprehension. It might help in the first sentence for the students to label the picture. Which figure is the tenant, which is the assistant, and which is the lieutenant? Underline ER, SS, TT, IEU, AR, EA, PP.
121	49-2	Suffixes ENT, EER	118	Slashes for syllables. Read the sentences together and have the students put them into their own words. "I'm sure the superintendant is against the current president because he wants to be elected himself." And "The engineer drives without pay because his real career is writing sonnets (poems of 14 lines, 10 syllables per line) and he writes better than any pioneer or mountain person." Underline double consonants, AR, OU, ER, EER.
122	50-1	Suffixes ITY, TY	119	Slashes. FEALTY means dedication to someone and LOYALTY is very similar. It means you are for someone and will always remain faithful to them...to have their back. The only sound to underline is OY in LOYALTY. All the other sounds can be heard on their own.
123	50-2	Suffix ARY	120	Slashes for syllables. Pay attention to word and sentence meanings. In the last sentence, the guy in the closet is the backup for the main speaker - in case the main speaker doesn't show up. Underline double consonants, OR, AR.
124	51	Suffixes ALLY, LY, WARD	121	Slashes and underline double consonants and TION, ARE, OO, SE, AR, CE, AI, OU, ER, EA. Identify Pinchy E and draw little curves. In column 1 at the top, look for the little words in the big words. IDEALLY has idea and ally. FINALLY has fin and ally. The suffix WARD means in that direction. In the direction of OUT or IN or UP, etc. LY suffix refers to how something was done, is word which tells us more about what is being done. CAREFULLY means done with care.
125	52	Suffix OUS	122	Slashes and underlining - AR, OR, ER, UR OU, EA, RR. AI. Suffix OUS means "has or with or full of." For example, HUMOROUS means with or full of humor. DANGEROUS means with or full of danger. Point out that OU is a sound spelling that appears frequently in our language. A reminder is to say "OH YOU!" These words are long but may be sounded out pretty easily when broken into syllables.
126	53	Suffixes CIOUS, TIOUS, SCIOUS	123	Slashes for syllables. Underline SC. In the first sentence, apparently the soup was pretty nasty and horrible. Note the flies buzzing around and the dead fish in the bowl! The person speaking in this sentence is pretty upset that the boy said it was delicious! With this suffix, use the phrase "I owe you" to help children remember the letter sequence.
127	51-1	Suffixes IOUS, CIOUS, TIOUS	124	Follow the same procedure as in the last few lessons. Focus on comprehension of the sentences. The words in this lesson are adjectives and the suffix means something like "full of." GLORIOUS means with or full of glory. CAUTIOUS means with or full of caution. Underline AR, UR, OR, AU, ER.
128	54-2	Suffix EOUS	125	Follow the same procedure as in the last few lessons. CONGRUOUS means the cars fit together nicely, ARDUOUS means difficult, IMPETUOUS means rash and AMBIGUOUS means not really clear. Underline OR, OUR, AR.

Target Sound Spelling:
Short a: /ă/ as in "at"

Use a yellow crayon to color the sound spelling for /ă/.

a /ă/

She **has** a **cat** who **ran** **at** my **ham** and **sat.**

I **had** to **ask,** "**Can** you **scat?**"

Fingermapping fig. 3 & 4

© 2010 Sarah K Major

Target Sound Spelling:
Short a: /ă/ as in "at"

Use a yellow crayon to color the sound spelling for /ă/.

a, au /ă/

In the
past, I
was **last.** Now
I'm **fast.**

Fran will
plan for
a **clan!**

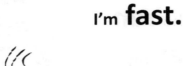

I **stand**
in the **sand**
to give the **grand**
band
a **hand!**

It's the best
in the **land!**

He will **laugh**

and **cough!***

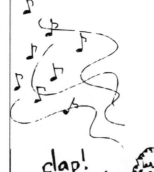

clap!
clap!
clap!

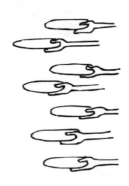

gh   au   I

*See also pg. 82

Fingermapping fig. 4 & 5

Target Sound Spelling:
Short e: /ĕ/ as in "red"

Use a yellow crayon to color the sound spelling for /ĕ/.

e /ĕ/

Don't **let** the **net** **get** **wet!**

Ned made a **red** **bed** for **Ted!**

He has **ten** in the **pen!**

Fingermapping fig. 3

© 2010 Sarah K Major

Name_____

**Target Sound Spelling:
Short e: /ĕ/ as in "red"**

Use a yellow crayon to color the sound spelling for /ĕ/.

e /ĕ/

The **p͟est** likes
to **r͟est** in
the **b͟est**
n͟est in
the **w͟est!**

**Tell
Nell**
the **b͟ell**
fell!

He b͟ent
the **t͟ent**
I **s͟ent.**

He f͟elt
the **p͟elt** on
his **b͟elt.**

Fingermapping fig. 4 and 6 (for "tell" etc.)

© 2010 Sarah K Major

Use a yellow crayon to color the sound spelling for /ĕ/.

ea, ai, ie /ĕ/

I **meant**
to have **bread**
ready for
breakfast.

I **spread** the
heavy
sweater to dry,
instead of
catching a **head** cold.

We're **friends**
to the end!

I **said**
again, I've
been **against** snakes!

Fingermapping fig. 7, 10 and 11. "ER is one sound /R/. Map compound words separately: break - fast.

© 2010 Sarah K Major

Name_____

Target Sound Spelling:
Short i: /ĭ/ as in "it"

Use a yellow crayon to color the sound spelling for /ĭ/.

i /ĭ/

See
if
it
is
in
its
big
pen.

Did
his
six
trick **him?**

Fingermapping fig. 3

© 2010 Sarah K Major

Use a yellow crayon to color the sound spelling for /ĭ/.

i /ĭ/

ı **still**
will
fill
the **grill**
with hotdogs.

ı **wish** we had
fish in our
dish!

ı **live**
to **give!**

Will **Nick**
pick
Rick to
lick
the **stick?**

Me? ME!

Fingermapping fig. 6 - each ending is 2 letters: LL, SH, VE, CK

7

© 2010 Sarah K Major

Name_____

Target Sound Spelling:
Short i: /ĭ/ as in "it"

Use a yellow crayon to color the sound spelling for /ĭ/.

i, ai, y, ui /ĭ/

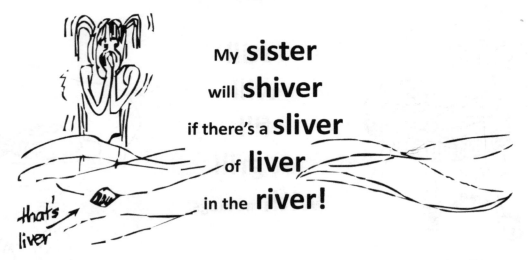

My **sister**
will **shiver**
if there's a **sliver**
of **liver**
in the **river!**

that's → liver

Captain is
certain to be
on the **mountain.**

That I have **rhythm** in
my **system** is a
myth!

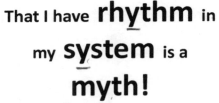

We will **build** again
what we **built** before.

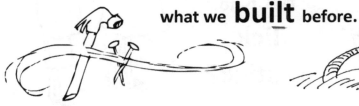

Fingermapping: ER, OU, AI, RH, TH, UI are one sound. Map multi-syllable words separately.

© 2010 Sarah K Major

Target Sound Spelling:
Short o: /ŏ/ as in "on"

Name_____

Use a yellow crayon to color the sound spelling for /ŏ/.

o /ŏ/

She **got**
on
and **off**
of
the slide.

Dot
got
hot
in her **cot.**

It's to **Tom**
from **Mom!**

Fingermapping fig. 3

© 2010 Sarah K Major

Name_____

Target Sound Spelling:
Short o: /ŏ/ as in "on"

Use a yellow crayon to color the sound spelling for /ŏ/.

o, *al /ŏ/

My **boss**
will **toss**
the **moss**
across.

We **lost.**
The **frost**
cost us.

The **long**
song
does not **belong.**
Be **strong!**

I ***walk**
and **talk**
with **chalk.**

*AL sound spelling.
Some people pronounce
the L in WALK. If you
do, teach this sound
spelling as just an A.

Fingermapping: SS, NG are one sound. Map multi-syllable words separately: be-long.

© 2010 Sarah K Major

Target Sound Spelling:
Short o: /ŏ/ as in "on"

Name_____

Use a yellow crayon to color the sound spelling for /ŏ/.

aw, a /ŏ/

I **saw** the **fawn**
on the **lawn**
yawn at
dawn.

It's the **law**
to **draw**
straws.

water

father

Father,
what I
want is
water!

I **was** going
to **watch** you
wash the dog.

Fingermapping: AW, TH, WH, TCH, SH, ER are one sound.

11

© 2010 Sarah K Major

Name_____

Target Sound Spelling:
Short o: /ŏ/ as in "on"

Use a yellow crayon to color the sound spelling for /ŏ/.

ough, ou, augh, au /ŏ/

I **thought**
they **ought**
to have **brought**
the candy they **bought**
and not have **fought** for more!

I have a **cough!**

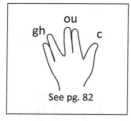

gh ou c

See pg. 82

STOP!!

I **caught** and
taught my
naughty
daughter.

August, said the
author, is
autumn.

I **haul**
because I like to!

Fingermapping: TH, OUGH, AUGH, ER, AU, MN, SE, OR are one sound. Map multi-syllable words separately if desired.

© 2010 Sarah K Major

Target Sound Spelling:
Short u: /ŭ/ as in "up"

Name_____

Use a yellow crayon to color the sound spelling for /ŭ/.

u /ŭ/

Come **up**
with **us**
and **run**
in the **sun!**

A --- choo!

We **just**
must
dust.

If you **jump**
you'll **bump**
the **grump!**

Grrrr

Fingermapping: all words are one letter per finger.

© 2010 Sarah K Major

Target Sound Spelling:
Short u: /ŭ/ as in "up"

Use a yellow crayon to color the sound spelling for /ŭ/.

u, oe, o /ŭ/

You **must** stay **under** the **bunk** **until** I say so!

Does it look done?

My **mother** and **brother** will go the **other** way.

Some boys will **come** and **shove** me high **above** the **dove** I **love**.

Fingermapping: ER, OE, TH, Consonant+E endings are one sound.

Target Sound Spelling:
Short u: /ŭ/ as in "up"

Name_____

Use a yellow crayon to color the sound spelling for /ŭ/.

ou, o, u, oo /ŭ/

The flood
was **rough**
and **tough**
enough
to **touch**
the whole **country**.

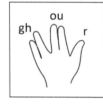

They are
coming, and
nothing will stop
them!

I **understand**
my **numbers** to
one **hundred**.

There was a **flood**
of **blood**
when I bumped my nose!

Fingermapping: OUGH, OU, NG, TH, ER, OO are one sound. Map multi-syllable words separately: under-stand.

© 2010 Sarah K Major

Target Sound Spelling:
Long a: /ā/ as in "ate"

Name_____

Use a yellow crayon to color the sound spelling for /ā/.

a-e /ā/

The **tame,**
lame dogs
came
to the **game**
and **ate.**

I will **bake**
a **cake**
to **take**
to the **lake.**

She has **lace**
about her **face.**

A **vase** is
in a **case**
at the **base.**

Fingermapping: all words have four fingers, but the 4th finger represent the Pinchy E. See page xiv.

**Target Sound Spelling:
Long a: /ā/ as in "ate"**

Name_____

Use a yellow crayon to color the sound spelling for /ā/.

ai, ay, ey /ā/

Don't **wait.**
The **rain**
will **stain**
the **daisy.**

I say,
"Today,
I **may**
stay and
play
all **day**
in the **spray!"**

I'll put my **bait**
in a **pail**
while I **wait**
for **Gail.**

They ↑
are my **prey.**

Fingermapping: figures 6&7. Two letter sounds include: AI, AY, TH, EY

© 2010 Sarah K Major

**Target Sound Spelling:
Long a: /ā/ as in "ate"**

Use a yellow crayon to color the sound spelling for /ā/.

ai, ay /ā/

Gail,
give us **aid**
with your
paintbrush!

The **plaintiff**
was **laid**
in **chains.**

The **mailman** on
the **mainland**
is **unpaid!**

Maybe
I should **always**
lay the
payment
away
in a **tray**.

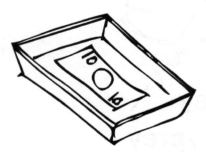

Fingermapping: AI, SH, FF, CH, AY are one sound. Map multi-syllable words separately: paint-brush.

© 2010 Sarah K Major

Target Sound Spelling:
Long a: /ā/ as in "ate"

Use a yellow crayon to color the sound spelling for /ā/.

ea, eigh, ei, aigh /ā/

Take a **break** for a **great steak!**

The **eight neighbors neigh** at the **weight** of the **freight** in the **sleigh!**

oh my aching back!
I want Mommy!
Waaa...
creak

In pain, they will go **straight** home!

She will **reign,** not **rein.**

She's so **vain,** she made a **vane** to show her **vein!**

Fingermapping: EY, EA, EI, EIGH, AIGH and GN (reign) are one sound. Map multi-syllable words separately: neigh-bors.

© 2010 Sarah K Major

Target Sound Spelling:
Long e: /ē/ as in "he"

Use a yellow crayon to color the sound spelling for /ē/.

e, ee, e-e /ē/

He,
me,
she,
(we) will
be there.

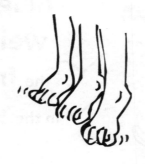

Do you **see?**
I **need**
to **keep**
my **three**
feet
green!

Even here,
Eve and
Pete
lose **these!**

Fingermapping: EE, TH, SH are one sound. Pinchy E page xiv section 8.

© 2010 Sarah K Major

Target Sound Spelling:
Long e: /ē/ as in "he"

Name_____

Use a yellow crayon to color the sound spelling for /ē/.

ee, ey, y, ea /ē/

The **sheep** on **sweet** **street** have **wheels** of **cheese.**

The **monkey** has the **key** to the **money!**

So **many** **funny** cats **only** come to the **city** to play!

I'll **eat** my **treat** on a **seat** by the **sea!**

Fingermapping: EE, SH, WH, CH, EY, NN, EA are one sound.

© 2010 Sarah K Major

Target Sound Spelling:
Long E: /ē/ as in "he"

Use a yellow crayon to color the sound spelling for /ē/.

ea /ē/

Oh **please** let me **dream** that you'll **really leave**!

Bea, please eat your **wheat** with **clean** hands, or you'll **grease** your **pleats!**

Fingermapping: EA, SE, VE, LL, WH are one sound. Silent E page xiv section 8.

**Target Sound Spelling:
Long E: /ē/ as in "he"**

Name_____

Use a yellow crayon to color the sound spelling for /ē/.

ie, ei /ē/

The **thief's**

mischief

caused **grief**

and **relief**

to the **chief.**

My fierce*
niece
did **achieve.**

I will **shriek**
as I **yield**
my **shield.**

* See R-Controlled
IER on page 68

Next she will

seize the

protein

and the **caffeine**

from the **ceiling.**

Fingermapping: TH, IE, CH, SH, FF, GN are one sound. Also CE, VE, NE endings.

© 2010 Sarah K Major

Name_____

Target Sound Spelling:
Long e: /ē/ as in "he"

Use a yellow crayon to color the sound spelling for /ē/, /ā/ & /ĭ/.

ei, eo, i, i-e /ē/

ı **seize**
some **leisure**
on my **weird**
ceiling.

ı **receive**
the **receipt**
with **conceit.**

Oh! So many **people!**

Maria
is so
petite!

Fingermapping: EI, PT, EO are one sound. Also ZE, NG, VE, TE, LE endings.

© 2010 Sarah K Major   24

Target Sound Spelling:
Long i: /ī/ as in "find"

Use a yellow crayon to color the sound spelling for /ī/.

i, y /ī/

The **child**
was **wild**,
not **mild!**

Eeeeeee Yaaaaah!!

I
find I
don't **mind**
if **I'm**
kind
in a **bind.**

Waah!

My kite
goes **by** me
in the **sky**
when I **try**
to **fly** it.
That is **why**
I will **cry!**

Fingermapping: CH, WH are one sound.

© 2010 Sarah K Major

Target Sound Spelling:
Long i: /ī/ as in "find"

Name_____

Use a yellow crayon to color the sound spelling for /ī/.

ie, i-e /ī/

I **cried** because

he **tried**

to **tie**

up the **pie**

I'd **fried**!

I got **five**

live

white

mice

while

he was by my

side!

We're **united!**

It's **time** for

you to **like**

your **life!**

Fingermapping: IE, WH are one sound. Pinchy E page xiv section 8.

© 2010 Sarah K Major

Target Sound Spelling:
Long i: /ī/ as in "find"

Name_____

Use a yellow crayon to color the sound spelling for /ī/.

igh, eigh, eye, is, ais /ī/

The **sigh** was **high.**

An **isle** is an **island**.

An **aisle** is in a church.

It's not **right** to **fight!**

I caught **sight** of a **bright** **light** in the **night** sky.

From his **height,** he could see everything!

I **might** get a **slight** **fright** **tonight.**

I see you with my **eyes!**

Fingermapping: IGH, IS, AIS, EIGH, EYE are one sound.

© 2010 Sarah K Major

Use a yellow crayon to color the sound spelling for /ō/.

o /ō/

Oh!
So it's
a **no**
go?

She **told** me
she'd **hold**
my **old**
gold,
but was **cold**
and **bold,**
and **sold** it!

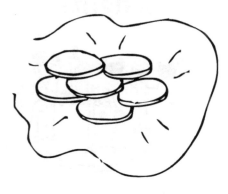

ı **also**
don't
want **both.**
Only that one!

Fingermapping: TH is one sound.

© 2010 Sarah K Major

28

Target Sound Spelling:
Long o: /ō/ as in "go"

Name_____

Use a yellow crayon to color the sound spelling for /ō/.

o-e, oo /ō/

Eat **more*** of the **core** **before** you go to the **store**.

*See more about R-Controlled ORE words on page 69.

Please **open** the door, then **close** it, and go **home!**

Still **over** the **smoke** was the **stroke** that **broke** the tree.

The **poor** **floor** is by the **door** to the **moor!**

Fingermapping: OO, ER are one sound. Pinchy E page xiv section 8.

© 2010 Sarah K Major

Target Sound Spelling:
Long o: /ō/ as in "go"

Use a yellow crayon to color the sound spelling for /ō/.

oa, ow /ō/

A **goat** in a **coat** will **float** on a **soap** **boat.**

I'll **toast** all the **loaf.**

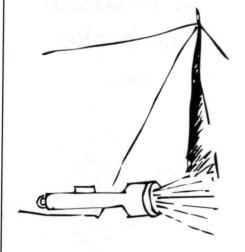

I'll **show** you the **low** **glow.**

You **know** I'll **throw** my **own** **snow** **below.**

Fingermapping: OA, OW, SH, KN, TH are one sound.

© 2010 Sarah K Major

Name_____

Target Sound Spelling:
Long o: /ō/ as in "go"

Use a yellow crayon to color the sound spelling for /ō/.

oe, ou, ough /ō/

A **doe** named **Poe** puts her **toe** on **Joe's** **hoe** as she **goes** by!

*You four? Your **souls,** of course are fine!

*See more about OUR spellings on page 71.

*I poured fourteen **potatoes** in the bowl.

Though and **although** are almost the same!

Fingermapping: OE, OU, OUGH, TH, OUGH are one sound. Map multi-syllable words separately: po-ta-toes.

© 2010 Sarah K Major

Name_____

Use a yellow crayon to color the sound spelling for /ū/.

u, u-e, ew, ue /ū/

It is **usual**
for a **pupil**
to **unite**
with friends.

I will **use**
a **fuse**
to get my
mule to move.

She will watch
for her **cue.**

Only a **few**
didn't say **ew!**
as they
ate the **stew!**

Fingermapping: UE, EW are one sound. Pinchy E page xiv section 8.

© 2010 Sarah K Major

32

Name_____

Use a yellow crayon to color the sound spelling for /sh/.

sh, ce /sh/

She will **shop** in the **ship** on the ocean.

The ship is on the **ocean.**

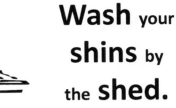

Wash your **shins** by the **shed.**

I **wish** the **fish** was a **shad.** It's a **sham!**

Fingermapping: SH, CE are one sound.

33

© 2010 Sarah K Major

Name_____

Target Sound Spelling:
/sh/ as in "she"

Use a yellow crayon to color the sound spelling for /sh/.

ss, s, ch, ci, sh /sh/

I **assure** you, the **issue** is no **tissue** for the **session**.

The machine is **sure** to make **sugar.**

The **chef** has a **chic machine** in the **chalet.**

Patricia made a **special, delicious** treat.

She gave a **short shout** at the **shoe show.**

I **shall** get **sharp shears** for **shaving.**

Fingermapping: spellings at top, center page are one sound. Map multi-syllable words separately: Pa-tri-cia.

© 2010 Sarah K Major

Target Sound Spelling: /th/ as in "the" & "with"

Use a yellow crayon to color the sound spelling for /th/.

th /th/

Eat more of

that
than
this.

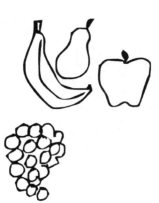

Put **both** of

them

in the

bath

with me.

Then
they

will play.

Fingermapping: TH, EY are one sound.

© 2010 Sarah K Major

Target Sound Spelling: /th/ as in "the" & "with"

Name_____

Use a yellow crayon to color the sound spelling for /th/.

th /th/

Yes, **these three** will get **those things!**

Mother and **father together** are **thick,** not **thin.**

I **think** I'll go see if **their** fir tree is still **there.**

The **moth** ate the **other cloth.**

Fingermapping: TH, EE, NG, ER, CK, NK, EIR, ERE are one sound. Map multi-syllable words separately: to-ge-ther.

Target Sound Spelling:
/ch/ as in "child"

Name_____

Use a yellow crayon to color the sound spelling for /ch/.

ch /ch/

Put **each**
chop on
your **chin.**

The **chaps** will
chat a bit
and **chow**
much.

The **child** got
such
a **chill!**

Fingermapping: EA, CH, OW, LL are one sound.

© 2010 Sarah K Major

Target Sound Spelling:
/ch/ as in "child"

Use a yellow crayon to color the sound spelling for /ch/.

tch, ch /ch/

Please **watch** that you **match** the **patch** on the **thatch.**

The **stitch** will **itch**, but I can't **scratch** it.

I'll **stretch** to **catch** the ball.

The **etch** a **sketch** is in the **ditch.**

I've a **hunch** the **bench** is in the **trench.**

Fingermapping: TH and spellings at top, center page are one sound.

© 2010 Sarah K Major

Target Sound Spelling:
/wh/ as in "when"

Name_____

Use a yellow crayon to color the sound spelling for /wh/.

wh /wh/

What hat?

when is Jen coming?

where is her chair?

which whip?

why fly?

are all good question words.

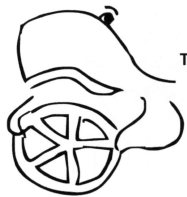

The **whale** is a
whiz at the
wheel,
I **whined.**

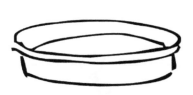

Please **whip** the
eggs for the cake.

Fingermapping: WH, CH, EE, ED are one sound. Silent E page xiv section 8.

39   © 2010 Sarah K Major

Target Sound Spelling:
/wh/ as in "when"

Name_____

Use a yellow crayon to color the sound spelling for /wh/.

wh /wh/

Whatever you do, **whisper,** don't **whoop,** while I **whittle** the **white whistle.**

Whenever you **whack** my **whirl** of **whiskers,** I **whimper.**

I wonder **whether** I will catch a **whopper whitefish.**

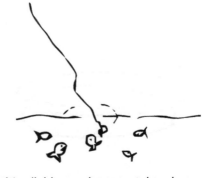

Fingermapping: TH, ER, OO, TT, ST, LE, CK, IR, ER, PP, SH are one sound. Map multi-syllable words separately: when-ever.

© 2010 Sarah K Major

Target Sound Spelling:
/oo/ as in "cool"

Use a yellow crayon to color the sound spelling for /oo/.

o, u, u-e /oo/

Do what

to

whom?

I'm **into**

"Do **unto** others

today, what you want for yourself."

Stu,

has the **flu.**

The **truth?**

Tulips are lovely!

It was

a **super**

flute!

Fingermapping: WH, AY, TH, ER are one sound.

© 2010 Sarah K Major

Target Sound Spelling:
/oo/ as in "cool"

Name_____

Use a yellow crayon to color the sound spelling for /oo/.

ou, o-e, oo, oe /oo/

You eat **soup** in a **group!**

Whose did you **lose** when you **moved?**

Mr. **Booth** has **balloons**, a **spoon**, **food**, and **boots**, too, but no **tooth!**

ha ha ha ha!

The **canoe** is a **shoe!**

Fingermapping: WH, OO, TH, LL, SE, ED, SH are one sound.

© 2010 Sarah K Major

Name_____

Target Sound Spelling:
/oo/ as in "cool"

Use a yellow crayon to color the sound spelling for /oo/.

ui, ew, ue, ough /oo/

The **suit** will **bruise** the **fruit**.

you & I

build

You and I will build.
You and I wear suits.
You and I like fruit.
You and I got a bruise.

Drew, there's **new** **dew** on the **stew!**

Sue, it's **true,** the **clue** was **blue** **glue.**

The birds **grew,** then **flew.**

I love blue glue!

blue glue

The glue is coming **through!**

Fingermapping: spellings at top, center page are one sound. Also SE.

© 2010 Sarah K Major

Target Sound Spelling:
/oo/ as in "cool"

Use a yellow crayon to color the sound spelling for /oo/.

oo, u-e, ough, ou, o-e, u /oo/

I have **proof.**
A **tablespoon**
is bigger than a
teaspoon.

I **assume**
you will **introduce**
me before you
conclude.
My **attitude**
is one of **gratitude.**

I'll go **through**
my **routine**
for **you.**

Do you
approve
my **moves?**

Yes, they
are very
fluid.

Fingermapping: LE, EA, TH, NE, PP, VE, SS, ME, CE, TT, DE are one sound. Silent E page xiv section 8.

© 2010 Sarah K Major

Use a yellow crayon to color the sound spelling for /oo/.

u, oo /oo/

I **put**
the **full**
bull
in the wagon.

Me?

Yup!

Now you **push**
or **pull** him!

I **took** a
good
look
at the
cook
book.

Fingermapping: LL, SH are one sound.

© 2010 Sarah K Major

Target Sound Spelling:
/oo/ as in "book"

Use a yellow crayon to color the sound spelling for /oo/.

oo, oul /oo/

The **crooked wooden footstool** sat on the **woolen** rug.

She **stood** by the **brook** and **shook.** My **goodness,** the **snook** is huge!

I **would** if I **could,** but you **should** clean up (not me!).

When I **looked,** I **mistook** him for a **crook!**

Fingermapping: SH, SS, ED are one sound.

Target Sound Spelling:
/oy/ as in "joy"

Use a yellow crayon to color the sound spelling for /oy/

 **oy, oi /oy/**

The **boy**
gave the **toy**
to **Joy**
and **Troy.**

I'll **point**
to the **coin**
in the
soil!

Let the **oil**
boil
in the
foil.

Fingermapping: OY, OI are one sound.

© 2010 Sarah K Major

Target Sound Spelling:
/oy/ as in "joy"

Name_____

Use a yellow crayon to color the sound spelling for /oy/

oy, oi /oy/

I **enjoy** a **loyal** **royal**.

Ahoy!
Don't **destroy** the **oyster** **decoy**!

I'll **join** in the **noise**!

His **voice** will **spoil** this **joint**.

I ran to **avoid** the **moist** **hoist**!

Fingermapping: OY, OI are one sound. Also SE, CE, ER.

© 2010 Sarah K Major

Target Sound Spelling:
/oy/ as in "joy"

Name_____

Use a yellow crayon to color the sound spelling for /oy/

oy, oi /oy/

The **destroyer** just **deployed.**

His **employment** was the **annoyment** of the **royalty** on the **voyage.**

There's **moisture** in the **adjoining** **cloister!**

The **boistrous** snake is **poisonous!**

This **joint** was your **choice!**

I'll **disappoint** you if I **embroider** this.

Fingermapping: NN, GE, OUS, CH, CE, ER, ED, URE, NG, PP Separate long words into syllables.

© 2010 Sarah K Major

Target Sound Spelling:
/ow/ as in "cow"

Name_____

Use a yellow crayon to color the sound spelling for /ow/

ow, ou /ow/

Wow,
how
the **SOW**
will **bow**
to the **COW**
now!

I will go
out and
about
our
house.

Fingermapping: OW, OU are one sound. Also SE ending.

© 2010 Sarah K Major

Target Sound Spelling: /ow/ as in "cow"

Name_____

Use a yellow crayon to color the sound spelling for /ow/

ow, ou /ow/

The **brown clown** will **frown downtown**.

Go **around** the **grounds outside without** me.

It will **shower** on the **flower**.

I'll give a **shout** when I've **found** the **stout mouse!**

Fingermapping: SH, ER, TH, SE are one sound. Pinchy E page xiv section 8.

© 2010 Sarah K Major

Target Sound Spelling:
/ow/ as in "cow"

Use a yellow crayon to color the sound spelling for /ow/

ou, ow, ough /ow/

The **amount** of **flour** in my **mouth** is a **mound**.

We will **plow** through the **crowded** vowels, however, the **prowler** got the **powder**.

I'm **bound** for the **sour** **mountain**.

There's a **drought** on the mountain.

Can you **pronounce** "**ounce** **couch?**"

I'll **allow** an **allowance** for the **coward** in the **tower**.

Fingermapping: TH, AI, ER, CE, CH, LL, AR are one sound. Separate long words into syllables.

© 2010 Sarah K Major

Target Sound Spelling:
/ng/ & /ngk/ as in
"king" & "wink"

Name_____

Use a yellow crayon to color the sound spelling for /ng/ & /nk/

ng /ng/

The **king**
will **ring** for
his **wing**
dings.

nk /ngk/

Wink at
the **pink**
ink in
the **sink.**

She **rang**
and **sang.**

Fingermapping: NG, NK are one sound.

© 2010 Sarah K Major

Target Sound Spelling:
/ng/ & /ngk/ as in
"king" & "wink"

Name_____

Use a yellow crayon to color the sound spelling for /ng/ & /nk/

/ng/

This **morning**
bring
string.

I want **nothing**
but a **spring**.

The bee **stung**

her nose as she

hung the wash.

nk /ngk/

I **think**
this **drink**
stinks!

The **bank**
stank and
the **tank**
sank.

The **bunk**
stunk.

Fingermapping: NG, NK, TH are one sound; two fingers.

© 2010 Sarah K Major

**Target Sound Spelling:
/ī/ & /ē/ as in "my" &
"funny"**

Name_____

Use a yellow crayon to color the sound spelling for y as /ī/ & /ē/

y /ī/

Try to
pry
my
ply off
the **sty.**

Oh no! It
will **fly**
by in
the **sky.**

y /ē/

I'm **happy**
very
many are
pretty.
Only two
jars of **cherry**
jelly
are **funny.**

Fingermapping: CH, ER, double letters are two fingers but one sound.

© 2010 Sarah K Major

Target Sound Spelling:
/ī/ & /ē/ as in "my" & "funny"

Use a yellow crayon to color the sound spelling for y as /ē/

y /ē/

Every family can **study quickly**.

Sorry! Don't **worry. Larry** can **carry** both the **muddy puppy** and the **funny bunny!** He'll **hurry!** They're **furry**.

The **cherry** is a **merry berry**.

Fingermapping: double letters and CK, ER, QU, CK, CH are two fingers but one sound.

Target Sound Spelling:
/er/ as in "her"

Use a yellow crayon to color the sound spelling for /er/

ir, er, or /er/

Sir,
the **girl**
will **stir**
the **fir.**

"Or" is a **word**
in **work**
and **worm.**

We **were**
to **serve**
her.

Fingermapping: RE, VE endings - 1 sound, 2 fingers.

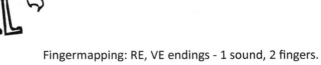

© 2010 Sarah K Major

Name_____

Target Sound Spelling:
/er/ as in "her"

Use a yellow crayon to color the sound spelling for /er/

ir, ur /er/

The **first** **girl** saw the **third** **bird** in the **dirt**.

It won't **hurt** to **turn** your **fur** in a **curl**.

She had a **shirt** and a **skirt** at the **circus**.

The **surf** will **churn** during the **storm**.

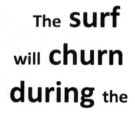

Fingermapping: TH, SH, CH, NG are two fingers but one sound.

Target Sound Spelling:
/er/ as in "her"

Name_____

Use a yellow crayon to color the sound spelling for /er/

ur, or, ear, er /er/

Okay, **return** the **turkey** or I'll **burst!**

I **heard** and will **learn** about the **early earth** in **earnest!**

Remember to **number** your **paper.**

Show **vigor!** The **armor** is **worse!**

Fingermapping: EY, EY, AR and sounds at top of page are two fingers but one sound.

© 2010 Sarah K Major

Name_____

Target Sound Spelling:
/er/ as in "her"

Use a yellow crayon to color the sound spelling for /er/

er, ear, our, ur /er/

I will **insert** my **concern** that he **deserve** the **service.**

hey!

Your **murmur** will **further** **disturb** my **current** **purpose.**

YAK YAK YAK YAK

He will **rehearse** the **search.**

The **tourist** showed **courage** on the **tour.**

Furnace Curtains

Before **curfew** I must **purchase** a **curtain** for my **furnace.**

Fingermapping: AI, CH, RR, CE, SE, GE, VE, TH and sounds at top of page are one sound.

© 2010 Sarah K Major

Target Sound Spelling:
/er/ as in "her"

Use a yellow crayon to color the sound spelling for /er/

ar, yr, ir, er /er/

I paid a **dollar** for this **collar!**

Oh, and I also got this **syrup.**

I can **confirm** that the **squirrel** will **circulate** around the **circular fir.**

I'm **alert** to **conserve** the **internal** and **external perfume.**

Fingermapping: LL, RR, VE and sounds at top of page are one sound.

© 2010 Sarah K Major

Target Sound Spelling:
/ar/ as in "star"

Name_____

Use a yellow crayon to color the sound spelling for /ar/

ar, ear /ar/

Art took the **cart** apart.

Smart Bart had a **tart** one from the **mart.**

Mark saw **stars** in the **park.**

He loves them with all his **heart.**

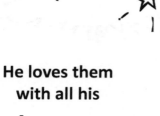

Fingermapping: Sounds at top of page are one sound but 2-3 fingers.

© 2010 Sarah K Major

Target Sound Spelling:
/ar/ as in "star"

Use a yellow crayon to color the sound spelling for /ar/

ar /ar/

The **alarm** will **start** the **party.**

Wear your **parka** and **scarf** to **art.**

I'm in **charge.** This **smart army** will **march** to the **market.**

Carla's **arms** **are** **large** and **scarlet.**

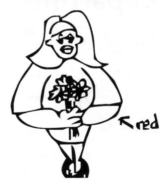

Fingermapping: AR, CH, GE are one sound.

© 2010 Sarah K Major

Target Sound Spelling:
/ar/ as in "star"

Use a yellow crayon to color the sound spelling for /ar/

ar, aur /ar/

Pardon my **remark** as I **guard** the **carpet.**

get lost!

The **apartment** is not **charming.** It is **starting** to be **alarming.**

You may **argue** the **harvest** **article** **farther** down. I **regard** my **department.**

hssss

hee haw! haw!

oink!

grrr

MY DEPARTMENT ♥

GO! GO!

Harvest Article

Fingermapping: AR, AUR, UA, CH, UE, ER, TH, LE, NG are one sound.

© 2010 Sarah K Major

Target Sound Spelling:
/air/ as in "vary"

Name_____

Use a yellow crayon to color the sound spelling for /air/

ere, eir, are, air /air/

Where is it?
There!

Pay the **fare**
for the **hare**
who will **care**
if he's **bare.**

The fir tree* is
their tree.

The **pair** will
take a **chair**
to the **fair** and
wear their **hair** in the **air**
with **flair.**

*"The fir" becomes "their"
when you lose the "f" from "fir."

Fingermapping: WH, TH, CH and sounds at top of page are one sound.

© 2010 Sarah K Major

Target Sound Spelling:
/air/ as in "vary"

Use a yellow crayon to color the sound spelling for /air/

ear, uar, are, air, ar /air/

The **bear** will **wear** the **pear** on his ear.

Don't **despair!** We will **repair** with **flair!**

And we **guarantee** our work!

I **declare!** Are you **aware?**

Does it **scare** you to **share?**

The **flare** I **prepare** for this **area** will **vary.**

It's **rare** for him to **spare** a **stare.**

Fingermapping: SH and sounds at top of page are one sound. Silent E page xiv section 8.

© 2010 Sarah K Major

Use a yellow crayon to color the sound spelling for /ear/

ere, eer /ear/

We're
here
in **cashmere.**

Cheer the
steer!

And don't **sneer** or
leer
at the **deer.**

I **peer**
at the **career**
pioneer.

Fingermapping: SH, CH and sounds at top of page are one sound. Silent E page xiv section 8.

© 2010 Sarah K Major

Name_____

Target Sound Spelling:
/ear/ as in "near"

Use a yellow crayon to color the sound spelling for /ear/

ear, ier /ear/

ᴵ **fear**
ₜₕₑ **tear**
ᵢₛ **near**
ₜₕₑ **rear**
₍ₒf ₜₕₑ **year.**

Please, **clear**
your **ear**
so you can **hear.**

I can see it
pierced ₜₕₑ
pier!

Fingermapping: ED and sounds at top of page are one sound.

© 2010 Sarah K Major

Target Sound Spelling:
/or/ as in "for"

Name_____

Use a yellow crayon to color the sound spelling for /or/

or, ore /or/

Don't forget.

Do your **chores**
before you go
to the **store.**

This **story** is
about a **tortoise**
named **Ivory** who
was **born** on
the **stormy**
shore.

Fingermapping: CH, OI and sounds at top of page are one sound. Silent E page xiv section 8.

© 2010 Sarah K Major

Target Sound Spelling:
/or/ as in "for"

Use a yellow crayon to color the sound spelling for /or/

or, ore /or/

The **hornet** stung the **stork** who tore the **acorn** on the **porch**.

The **storm** is in the **north** **corner** this **morning**.

Don't **forget** to **order** the **form**.

She **tore** what she **wore** before she got to **score** more.

Fingermapping: ER, CH, TH, NG and sounds at top of page are one sound.

© 2010 Sarah K Major

Target Sound Spelling:
/or/ as in "for"

Use a yellow crayon to color the sound spelling for /or/

ar, oor, our /or/

My arm
was too **warm**
in the **war.**

The **poor**
door is on the
floor.

The
***tourist**
shows
courage
on the
tour.

Your
fourth will
pour.

And, of
course,
your
four
gourds are
on the
court!

*See also OUR /ER/ spellings page 60.
Depending on pronunciation, teach
OUR words as /OR/ or /ER/.

Fingermapping: TH, GE, SE and sounds at top of page are one sound.

© 2010 Sarah K Major

Use a yellow crayon to color the sound spelling for /or/

or, ore /or/

I **adore**
the **foreman**
with **authority**
over the **territory.**
Therefore,
ignore
my **mortar.**

"or" and "ore" are mixed together.

I will **forever**
have the **fortune**
of an **enormous**
ornament.

I **inform**
the **force**
to be **formal**
as they **perform**
the **important**
play.

Fingermapping: TH, AU, RR, ER, OU, AR, CE, NE, OUS and sounds at top of page are one sound.

© 2010 Sarah K Major

Name_____

Use a yellow crayon to color the sound spelling for /s/ & /j/

ce /s/

g(e), g(i), g(y)
-ge /j/

Grace
will **place** the
lace about
her **face.**

Gem,
a **large**
gentle
genie,
wears **gel.**

There's a **giant**
giraffe
by the **gym.**

Fingermapping: AR, IE, LE, FF are one sound. Silent E page xiv section 8.

© 2010 Sarah K Major

UNIT 26
LEVEL 2

Name_____

**Target Sound Spelling:
Soft C & G as in "cent"
and "gem"**

Use a yellow crayon to color the sound spelling for /s/ & /j/

c(e), c(i), -ce /s/

-ge, dge /j/

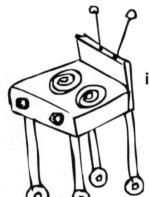

The **range** is **strange.**

It's **nice** to **dance** in the **center** of the **space** for **once.**

I need my **badge** so I'll **dodge** to the **lodge** on the **ridge** by the **bridge.**

Draw a **circle** around the **city** **circus** with your **pencil.**

city circus

lodge

Fingermapping: DG, ER, IR, LE are one sound.

Target Sound Spelling: Soft C & G as in "cent" and "gem"

Use a yellow crayon to color the sound spelling for /s/ & /j/

c(e), c(y) /s/

The **cell**
in the **cemetery**
has a **ceiling**
of **cement.**

The **cyclops**
has a **cycle** with one
cylindar.

dge /j/

Mercy,
the **cent**
is a **century**
old!

Judge, Bud
will eat **fudge**
as he's **wedged**
in the **hedge**
on the **edge**
of the **ledge.**

Fingermapping: LL, ER, EI, LE, AR, UR, DG are one sound. Map long words by syllable.

© 2010 Sarah K Major

Target Sound Spelling:
Soft C & G as in "cent" and "gem"

Name_____

Use a yellow crayon to color the sound spelling for soft c & g

ce /s/

g(i), ge, g(y) /j/

My **stance**
on **France**
is that for
romance
they **dance**
and **prance.**

A **package**
by the **cottage** was the
cabbage
for the **village.**

The **gigantic**
magic
giant does
gymnastics
with the **gymnast.**

I see your
courage
with the
baggage.

Fingermapping: CK, TT, BB, LL, OUR, GG are one sound. Silent E page xiv section 8. Map long words by syllable page xiv.

© 2010 Sarah K Major

Name_____

Use a yellow crayon to color the double consonants in each word.

For **dinner**
or **supper**
in the **summer,**
pepper
is **better!**

He left the **letter**
on the **ladder!**

Our **lesson**
today is on **cotton**
ribbon.

Otto is on the **bottom.**

It was **sudden!**
It did **happen!**
The **kitten**
lost her **mitten!**

Fingermapping: double consonants and ER are one sound.

77

© 2010 Sarah K Major

Double consonants with short vowels & single consonants with long vowels.

Name_____

Use a yellow crayon to color the double consonants in each word. The words with long vowel sounds have only one consonant in the middle of the word. Color the consonant in the middle of the words.

I **grinned** and **tapped** as I **wrapped.**

I'm **grinning** and **tapping** and **wrapping.**

I'm **joking** about **saving** my gum.

I **cared** that she's so **caring** and **smiled** to see her **smiling!**

I **fixed** mine; he's **fixing** his.

Fingermapping: NG, WR, ED and double consonants are one sound.

© 2010 Sarah K Major

Double consonants

Use a yellow crayon to color the double consonants in each word.

I will **affirm** that I can **afford** to **affix** a stamp.

I will be **attentive** to my **attire** as I **attempt** to **attain** the prize.

She will **assert** her ability to **assemble** an **assortment** of **assets**.

According to this **account,** we have the **assurance** of our **accustomed** payment.

I **applaud** in my **approval** to his **application** at the **appliance** store. He has the **appetite** for this work.

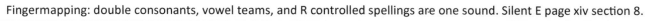

Fingermapping: double consonants, vowel teams, and R controlled spellings are one sound. Silent E page xiv section 8.

© 2010 Sarah K Major

Color the schwa at the beginning of each word.

a /uh/

I see you are **asleep.**

I'm **about**

to go out and I'm

afraid it will rain

again.

I see the one **above** is

awake.

Awhile

ago it was

alive. I saw it go

away--

ahead

around and

about the barn.

IT

Fingermapping: long vowel spellings and diphthongs are one sound. Also, WH, VE and Pinchy E spellings.

© 2010 Sarah K Major

Target Sound Spelling:
/f/ as in "fun"

Use a yellow crayon to color the sound spelling for /f/

ff /f/

The **traffic**
waffled
and **baffled**
me, so an **officer**
offered
to make an **effort**
to **effect**
a **difficult** change.

No fun!

I will **affirm** him!

Fingermapping: FF, ED, ER, OR, IR are one sound.

© 2010 Sarah K Major

Target Sound Spelling:
/f/ as in "fun"

Use a yellow crayon to color the sound spelling for /f/

ph, gh /f/

Phil will **phone** for the **photos.**

gh ou r

I am **rough** and **tough** **enough!**

gh au l

He will **laugh** and **cough** both!

Phew! **Phil's** **phony** **phase** with **phlox** is over!

I see a **phrase** in our **phonics** book.

Phonics — down the hill

Phrases — run and jump

Fingermapping: PH, EW, GH, AU are 2 letter sound spellings. Watch for Pinchy E spellings.

© 2010 Sarah K Major

Lightning Source UK Ltd.
Milton Keynes UK
UKHW05f2053171018
330725UK00025B/443/P

9 780982 987308

Target Sound Spelling:
/f/ as in "fun"

Use a yellow crayon to color the sound spelling for /f/

ph, gh /f/

Play the
phonograph
for the **elephant**
at the **pharmacy.**

The **physician**
needs more **phloem***
for the **pharmacy.**

Pharaoh saw
a **phantom**
pheasant*
by **Pharos!****

Orpheus,
the **orphan**
sophomore
will **triumph**

musically!

I have a
phobia about
philomels* and
phoebes.**

*phloem= part of trunk that
carries food to the rest of the
tree.
**Pharos - an ancient lighthouse
built on the island of Pharos.
***pheasant, philomels, &
phoebes are birds.

Fingermapping: PH, GH are one sound. Also ORE, OE, EA. Map words a syllable at a time.

© 2010 Sarah K Major

Target Sound Spelling:
/g/ as in "got"

Use a yellow crayon to color the sound spelling for /g/

g, gg, gh /g/

Words like **ghastly,**
ghoul,
and **ghost**
scare me!

The **baggy gaggle**
of geese will **wiggle**
and **struggle.**

In the **ghetto**
in **Ghana**
and **Ghent***,
people eat **gherkins**
dipped in **ghee****
while sitting on the
ghat*.

The **girls**
got sick,
gave a **great**
groan, and are
going home.

*NW Belgium
**Indian strained liquid butter
***In India, steps to water where
people do ritual bathing

Fingermapping: ER, IR, EE, LE, EA, OA, NG are one sound. Map words a syllable at a time. See page xiv.

© 2010 Sarah K Major

Target Sound Spelling:
/k/ as in "kiss"

Name_____

Use a yellow crayon to color the sound spelling for /k/

c, ck, k /k/

Bad **luck** – when I'm **sick,** I can't **kick.**

I **cast** my **cake** in a **cave.**

I'll **lock** the **rock** by the **dock.**

Don't **tackle** **Jack.**

Take a **look** at the **cook.**

I see a **pike** on a **bike.**

Don't **kiss** the **kite.**

Fingermapping: CK, OO, SS are one sound. Also LE and Pinchy E.

© 2010 Sarah K Major

Name_____

Target Sound Spelling:
/k/ as in "kiss" /kw/
as in queen

Use a yellow crayon to color the sound spelling for /k/

ck, ch, k, c /k/   qu /kw/

Give it a **quick crack.**

At the **park,** I will **skin** my knee this **week.**

Oh! **Quit,** or the **queen** will give the **quart** a **quick squeeze**.

There was **magic music** at the **second picnic.**

Chris has no **school** at **Christmas.**

Fingermapping: EE, OO, AR, ZE are one sound. Map words a syllable at a time. See page xiv.

© 2010 Sarah K Major

Target Sound Spelling:
/l/ as in "left"

Name_____

Use a yellow crayon to color the sound spelling for /l/

l, ll, il /l/

A **lift**
will **land**
me in the **left**
loft where
I will **lie.**

The **pupil**
is **ill.**

I **will**
sell
the **full**
doll in
the **mall**
at the **well.**

Fingermapping: ll, IE are one sound. See figure 6, page xii.

© 2010 Sarah K Major

Target Sound Spelling:
/l/ as in "left"

Name_____

Use a yellow crayon to color the sound spelling for /l/

le, al /l/

All the **simple**
little
purple
people love
to **sample**
a **maple**
apple.

Al's **rural**
sabal
is **natural.**

In **general,**
I'm **loyal**
to the **final**
normal
rural
festival.

Farmer's Market
Last one this year.

Fingermapping: TT, UR, EO, PP, OY, OR, UR are one sound. Map words a syllable at a time. See page xiv.

© 2010 Sarah K Major

Target Sound Spelling:
/l/ as in "left"

Use a yellow crayon to color the sound spelling for /l/

el, il /l/

The **angel** will **counsel** the **panel** to not **marvel** at the **label** on the **parcel.**

The **pupil** took the **fossil** to the **civil** **council.**

Fingermapping: OU, AR, SS, OU are one sound. Map longer words a syllable at a time. See page xiv.

© 2010 Sarah K Major

Target Sound Spelling: /l/ as in "left"

Name_____

Use a yellow crayon to color the sound spelling for /l/

al, le /l/

My **central**
rival is a
typical gal:
practical,
rational and
neutral.

An **isle**∗
is a **little** island.

An **aisle**∗

is in a church.

∗is and ais /i/

Fingermapping: Section 6 letter clusters page xiii and Section 8 multi-syllable words page xiv.

© 2010 Sarah K Major   90

Target Sound Spelling:
/m/ as in "my"

Use a yellow crayon to color the sound spelling for /m/

mn, mb /m/

Sing an **autumn hymn.**

I'd **comb** my **lamb,** but my **thumb** is **numb.**

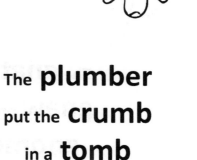

We were **solemn** by the **column** where they will **condemn** him.

The **plumber** put the **crumb** in a **tomb** with great **aplomb.**

Fingermapping: Section 6 letter clusters page xiii and Section 8 multi-syllable words page xiv.

© 2010 Sarah K Major

Target Sound Spelling:
/n/ as in "not"

Use a yellow crayon to color the sound spelling for /n/

kn, gn, pn /n/

I **know** that my **gnat** has **pneumonia!**

I **knew** that the **knife** was in the **knapsack** by my **knee.**

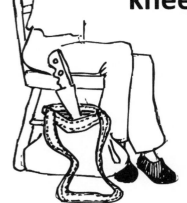

The **gnat** will **gnaw** on the **gnome.**

I **knit** him some **knickers.**

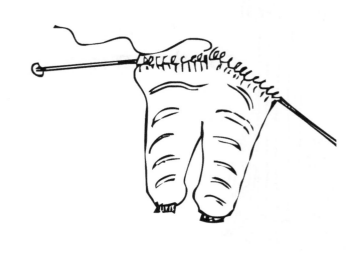

Fingermapping: Section 6 letter clusters page xiii and Section 8 multi-syllable words page xiv.

Target Sound Spelling:
/r/ as in "ran"

Use a yellow crayon to color the sound spelling for /r/

rh, wr /r/

A **rhino**
has no **rhythm**
and can't **rhyme.**

um   uh   duh

The **wren**
will **write**
what I **wrote**
with the **wrong**
wrist.

Rhoda left
Rhode Island for
Rhodesia to look
for a **rhebok.**

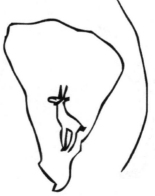

Fingermapping: Section 6 letter clusters page xiii and Section 8 multi-syllable words page xiv.

© 2010 Sarah K Major

Use a yellow crayon to color the sound spelling for /r/

rh, wr /r/

At the **Rhyne,**
she saw a **rhesus**
with **rheumatism**
digging up **rhizomes.**

To **wrangle** means to
argue with **wrath.**

Rhetoric
and **rhapsody**

go well together.

The **wringer**
will **wrinkle** the pants.

Fingermapping: Section 6 letter clusters page xiii and Section 8 multi-syllable words page xiv.

Name_____

Target Sound Spelling:
/r/ as in "ran"

Use a yellow crayon to color the sound spelling for /r/

rh, wr /r/

Her garden is a **rhombus** where she planted **rhododendrons** and **rhubarb.**

Mr. **Wright,** a **wrangler,** got a **wrench** to fix the **wretched** **wreck.**

The **wraith** will **wrestle** with the **wrapping** on the **wreath.**

Fingermapping: Section 6 letter clusters page xiii and Section 8 multi-syllable words page xiv.

© 2010 Sarah K Major

Use a yellow crayon to color the sound spelling for /s/

st, sc /s/

Listen!
She will **whistle**
but her **bustle**
will **rustle**
in the **castle.**

There are **scent** and
scissors
in **science.**

On the **Scilly**
Isles the **scion**
has a **scimitar**
that **scintillates**
in the sun.

Fingermapping: Section 6 letter clusters page xiii and Section 8 multi-syllable words page xiv.

© 2010 Sarah K Major

Target Sound Spelling:
/s/ as in "sit"

Use a yellow crayon to color the sound spelling for /s/

ce, ci, cy, se /s/

They **conceal** the **cereal** and **celery** at the **grocery** store.

Practice to **recite** at the **cinema.**

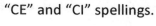

"CE" and "CI" spellings.

Let's **celebrate** your **recent** ... **exercise.**

"CE" and "CI" spellings.

The **cyclops** has a **fancy** **cylindar.**

He says a **horse** is **worse!**

Fingermapping: Section 6 letter clusters page xiii and Section 8 multi-syllable words page xiv.

© 2010 Sarah K Major

Target Sound Spelling:
/t/ as in "tap"

Name_____

Use a yellow crayon to color the sound spelling for /t/

ed, tt /t/

ı **passed**

him the pants I

pressed.

I'm **putting**

a **pretty**

button

on the **kitten's**

mitten.

ı **asked**

before I **looked.**

I'll **attempt** to

be **attentive** in

my **attendance**

at school.

It **matters**!

Fingermapping: Section 6 letter clusters page xiii and Section 8 multi-syllable words page xiv.

© 2010 Sarah K Major

Target Sound Spelling:
/t/ as in "tap"

Name_____

Use a yellow crayon to color the sound spelling for /t/

bt, pt /t/

I **doubt**

he will be **subtle**

about **debt.**

Ptolemy[3] drank

ptisan[4] and got

ptomaine

poisoning and then

ptosis[5].

The **ptarmigan**[1]

and **pterodactyl**

are friends who eat

pteropods[2].

1 ptarmigan: an alpine grouse

2 pteropod: small shell-less gastropod that swims by means of winged lobes

3 Ptolemy: a man who thought that the solar system rotated around the earth

4 ptisan: a drink made of barley

5 ptosis: the falling of an organ, such as a droopy eye

Fingermapping: Section 6 letter clusters page xiii and Section 8 multi-syllable words page xiv.

© 2010 Sarah K Major

Name_____

Target Sound Spelling:
/z/ as "zoo"

Use a yellow crayon to color the sound spelling for /z/

se, ze, ss, s, x /z/

Phil's new **phase** is to **pause** to **browse.**

The visitor left the **scissors** at school.

If you **lose,** you will **arise** and **tease** each one on the **cruise.**

My **husband** is filled with **optimism** not **pessimism** about **his visitor.**

The **freeze** will **amaze** me so that I can't **snooze!**

The X in **xylophone** sounds like a Z.

Fingermapping: Section 6 letter clusters page xiii and Section 8 multi-syllable words page xiv.

© 2010 Sarah K Major

Target Sound Spelling:
/off/, /uf/ & /oh/
6 sounds of ough

Name_____

Use a yellow crayon to color the sound spelling for /off/, /uf/ & /oh/

ough /off/, /oh/, /uf/

He will **cough**

in the

trough.

Fingermapping: OU-GH sounds like "O-FF"

It's true **though.**
Although I went,

I never got there.

Fingermapping: OUGH sounds like "OH"

He was **rough**
and **tough**
enough
to **slough** off

all the others.

Fingermapping: OU-GH sounds like "U-FF"

© 2010 Sarah K Major

Target Sound Spelling:
/oo/, /ow/ & /ŏ/
6 sounds of ough

Name_____

Use a yellow crayon to color the sound spelling for /oo/, /ow/ & /ŏ/

ough /oo/, /ow/, /ŏ/

The snake crawled

through

the word.

Fingermapping: OUGH sounds like "OOO"

The **bough**
in the **slough**
had a **drought.**

Fingermapping: OUGH sounds like "OW"

Meet the Ought Brothers!

They **thought**

they **ought**

to have **brought**

the candy they

bought

and not have **fought**

for more.

Fingermapping: OUGH sounds like short O

© 2010 Sarah K Major

**Target Sound Spelling
Past Tense:
/t/, /d/ & /ed/**

Name_____

Use a yellow crayon to color the sound spelling for /t/, /d/ & /ed/

ed /t/, /d/, /ed/

I **tripped**
then **slipped**
and **dropped** it.
So I **stopped**.

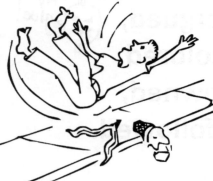

She was **charmed**
that I **farmed**.

As I **tilled**,
I **filled** the cart.

I **wanted**
Ed, and I **spotted**
him.

I **rubbed**
as I **planned**.

We **strayed**
as we **played**.

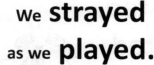

I said it **needed**
to be **weeded**
and **planted**
and **painted**
and **dusted**.
I just **waited**.

Fingermapping: Double letters are one sound. ED /T/ is one sound, ED /D/ is one sound.

© 2010 Sarah K Major

**Target Sound Spelling
Past Tense:
/t/, /d/ & /ed/**

Name_____

Use a yellow crayon to color the sound spelling for /t/, /d/ & /ed/

ed /t/, /d/, /ed/

I have **cracked,
tracked,
chopped,
wrapped,
mocked,
baked,
walked,**
and **talked.**

I was busy yesterday!

**I cleaned,
adored,
argued,
colored,
owned,**
and **followed.**

Note: The e in "ed" cannot act as "pinchy e" if there are two consonants between it and the vowel (as in "tracked"), nor in the case of "bossy R" ("or" or "er" as in "colored" and "adored"), nor when the previous vowel sound is made of two vowels together as in "treated."

I also **headed,
coasted,
drifted,
boasted,
wasted,**
and **treated**

Ed pretty badly.

Fingermapping: Double letters are one sound. ED /T/ is one sound, ED /D/ is one sound.

Target Sound Spelling
Past Tense:
/d/ & /ed/

Name_____

Use a yellow crayon to color the sound spelling for /d/ & /ed/

ed /d/, /ed/

They **remained** in the rain and **complained** until they **obtained** umbrellas.

Ed **directed;** what **resulted** is that he **profited.**

We **differed;** he **excelled.**

I **admitted** that I **permitted** it.

I **wondered** who **restored** the **soiled** vase.

Fingermapping: Section 6 letter clusters page xiii and Section 8 multi-syllable words page xiv.

© 2010 Sarah K Major

+s

The **girls** saw **eggs** turn to **birds.**

Boys in **sneakers** had **boats** and **trucks.**

The **cars** have **firs.**

+es

She **wishes** for **dishes,** but got **foxes** in **boxes.**

He wears **glasses** in his **classes.**

Fingermapping: Section 6 letter clusters page xiii.

--ies

I have **memories**
of **parties**
where I ate **candies**
and told **stories.**

My **puppies**
eat a lot of **groceries.**

These **diaries**
tell of **treaties**
with other **countries.**

--s

These
characters
put **essays**
in **envelopes.**

The **chiefs**
wear **badges**
in the **palaces**
in the **valleys.**

v+es

The **wolves**
cut **loaves**
into four **halves.**

Fingermapping: Section 8 multi-syllable words page xiv. Map endings: IE-S /E-Z/, ES /E-Z/, V-ES /V-Z/

107

© 2010 Sarah K Major

__o --> es

The **mosquitoes** love the **potatoes** and **tomatoes** that grow by the **volcanoes**.

s inside

The **passers-by** are **mothers-in-law** and **fathers-in-law**.

f --> v-es

The **shelves** were full of **knives** the **thieves** didn't see.

s outside

The **mix-ups** were about **teaspoonfuls**, **spoonfuls** and **cupfuls**.

y --> ie-s

The **opportunities** for **activities** in **companies** have no **boundaries**.

Fingermapping: Section 6 letter clusters page xiii and Section 8 multi-syllable words page xiv.

UNIT 42

Name_____

Special Endings
n, en

Add **n***

broken
shaken
awaken
stolen
frozen

Add **en****

frighten
straighten

Add **consonant + en*****

flatten
forgotten

* Pinchy e makes first vowel long so only
need to add an n.

** Add an en to words which 1) don't have
a final e and
2) have multiple final
consonants

*** Must double final consonant + add en
if the vowel before final consonant is short.
Double consonant will keep the e in en
from pinching first vowel.

Fingermapping: Section 6 letter clusters page xiii and Section 8 multi-syllable words page xiv.

© 2010 Sarah K Major

Special Endings
ish, ist, ize

ish, ist, ize

He's acting **childish,**
foolish
and **selfish!**

I know a **scientist**
colonist,
an **artist**
tourist,
and a **typist**
cyclist.

Her gown is **bluish**
and **stylish.**

I **realize**
I need to **organize,**
memorize,
specialize
and **summarize,**
so don't **criticize**
as I **civilize**
and **fertilize** this farm.

Fingermapping: Section 6 letter clusters page xiii and Section 8 multi-syllable words page xiv.

© 2010 Sarah K Major

**Special Endings
or, er**

or

**Actor/
Director**

**Instructor/
Professor**

**Inventor/
Operator**

**Editor/
Creditor**

The **mayor,
senator,**
and **governor**
love to **motor.**

er

The **passenger**
is either a **commander,**
or a **pitcher**
and **publisher,**
or a **homemaker/
gardener.**

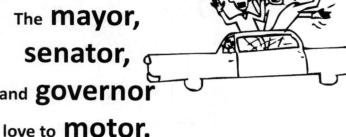

Fingermapping: Section 6 letter clusters page xiii and Section 8 multi-syllable words page xiv.

© 2010 Sarah K Major

ion

My **profession**
is a **companion**
with a **solution**
I can **mention.**

My **mission**
is to **section**
a **million** onions.

ian

The **librarian**
has a **comedian**
for a **custodian.**

The **electrician**
is a **guardian**
to the **musician.**

Fingermapping: Section 6 letter clusters page xiii and Section 8 multi-syllable words page xiv.

© 2010 Sarah K Major

UNIT 45
Level 2

Name_____

Special Endings
sion /zhun/
tion, sion, cian /shun/

sion /zhun/

tion, sion, cian /shun/

The **vision**
on **television**
was a **collision**,
then an **emersion**.

Our **mission**
is **suspension**
in another **dimension**.

I'm on **vacation**
at a **plantation**
to get an **explanation**
of the **election**
in our **nation**.

Yes! See I that Ann is a
physician
and a **musician**.

Fingermapping: Section 6 letter clusters page xiii and Section 8 multi-syllable words page xiv.

© 2010 Sarah K Major

Special Endings
sure /zhur/
ture /cher/

sure /zhur/

What a **pleasure**
to, at **leisure**,
measure
the **treasure**.

ture /cher/

Go **gesture**
and **posture**
about **nature**
in the **pasture**.

Your new **adventure**
is to **capture**
the **future**
furniture
structure.

Fingermapping: Section 6 letter clusters page xiii and Section 8 multi-syllable words page xiv.

© 2010 Sarah K Major

cia, tia /shu/

Marcia
made **Patricia**
a **facia** for her shop.

sia /zhu/

Asia
went to **Persia**
to buy a **freesia**,
but got **amnesia** instead.

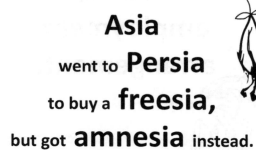

The **consortia's**
inertia
was due to **dementia.**

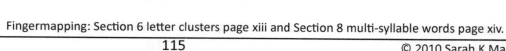

Fingermapping: Section 6 letter clusters page xiii and Section 8 multi-syllable words page xiv.

115

© 2010 Sarah K Major

Special Endings
ment, mate, rate, ness

ment, ate, ness

To my **amusement** the **argument** was over my **employment arrangement.**

The **ultimate** cure was **unfortunate,** but it *was* **immediate.**

I love the **swiftness** of his **gentleness** in her **sickness.**

You're **accurate.** I'm **desolate** and **desperate.**

It's **fortunate** that he'll **moderate** the **delicate** meeting.

Fingermapping: Section 6 letter clusters page xiii and Section 8 multi-syllable words page xiv.

© 2010 Sarah K Major

ant

The **tenant**
is a **servant**
of the **assistant**
to the **attendant**
of the **lieutenant.**

The **applicant**
saw the **participant**
merchant.

The **vacant**
house was **radiant**
and **pleasant.**

Fingermapping: Section 6 letter clusters page xiii and Section 8 multi-syllable words page xiv.

© 2010 Sarah K Major

I am **confident** it is no **accident** that the **superintendent** is the **ardent** **opponent** of the **resident** **president.**

The **volunteer** **engineer** is a **career** **sonneteer** and can **outsteer** any **pioneer** or **mountaineer.**

Fingermapping: Section 6 letter clusters page xiii and Section 8 multi-syllable words page xiv.

© 2010 Sarah K Major

ity, ty

For the **majority** of **humanity**, **humidity** hurts their **vanity**.

She has the **ability** to use her **creativity** to make an **activity** that needs **agility**.

Fealty and **loyalty**... each is my **specialty**.

Fingermapping: Section 6 letter clusters page xiii and Section 8 multi-syllable words page xiv.

119

© 2010 Sarah K Major

ary

It's **necessary**
to have a **momentary**
voluntary rest.

I'm not **solitary;**
I've an **ordinary**
imaginary friend.

It's **customary**
to have a **temporary**
honorary
secondary backup.

Fingermapping: Section 6 letter clusters page xiii and Section 8 multi-syllable words page xiv.

Name_____

ally, ly, ward

Ideally,

Ally will have an

idea for a fin **finally.**

Additionally,

she'll be **especially**

quick to make it.

I'm tired!

I went **outward,**

inward,

upward,

skyward, even,

and **afterward**

went **eastward**

and finally **homeward!**

We are **barely**

awake, but **loosely,**

not **carefully,**

we're running **directly**

home, **scarcely**

seeing it will **certainly**

rain. **Possibly**

we will be

completely

wet!

Fingermapping: Section 6 letter clusters page xiii and Section 8 multi-syllable words page xiv.

© 2010 Sarah K Major

Name_____

ous /us/

It was **marvelous** to hear the **humorous,** **famous** actor talk of his **vigorous,** **dangerous,** **adventurous** trips in **wondrous** **mountainous** lands.

It was **fabulous** not to be **jealous.** I'd be **nervous** in **various** **tremendous** and **horrendous** climbs on **stupendous** mountain peaks.

Fingermapping: Section 6 letter clusters page xiii and Section 8 multi-syllable words page xiv.

Name_____

c
t — ious /shus/
sc

xious /kshus/

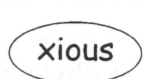
xious

It was **precocious,**
malicious,
atrocious,
and **ferocious,**
to say this is **delicious**
and then remain
conscious.

Better be **anxious**
than **obnoxious.**

tious

Teach the phrase "I owe you" to help
students remember the spelling pattern.
Once those spelling patterns are identified,
the rest of the sounds are simple.

It is **fictitious**
that this is **nutritious.**

Fingermapping: Section 6 letter clusters page xiii and Section 8 multi-syllable words page xiv.

© 2010 Sarah K Major

ious /eeus/, /shus/

I'm **industrious**

and **studious**

as I work on the **tedious**

lessons.

It's **obvious**

that **various**

curious

fellows are **cautious**

about the class.

On a **precious,**
glorious

Saturday they'd be **furious**

to have to study.

Mom says this **mysterious**

soup is **nutritious.** Hmm.

NOTES:
tious and cious sound
like "shus."

Vowels in this ending
spell out
"I owe you."
i o u

Fingermapping: Section 6 letter clusters page xiii and Section 8 multi-syllable words page xiv.

© 2010 Sarah K Major   124

Special Endings
eous /ē-ŭs/
uous /ū-ŭs/

eous /ē-ŭs/

It is **advantageous** to be **gorgeous,** **courteous,** and **courageous...** but not **contageous.**

uous /ū-ŭs/

The line of cars is **congruous** and **continuous.**

The climb is **arduous** and the **impetuous** conductor was **ambiguous** about his speed.

Fingermapping: Section 6 letter clusters page xiii and Section 8 multi-syllable words page xiv.

© 2010 Sarah K Major

No **way,**

not today!

I can't

weigh

eight sleighs!

Will you **sell**

your bike?

The **cell**

is in the cellar.

Its leg is broken.

It's about to sneeze!

It's **great**

to eat steak! She ate

the cheese I wanted to

grate.

Gail made a **sail.**

Dale had a **sale.**

You **owe** me!

Oh yeah?

Fingermapping: Section 6 letter clusters page xiii and Section 8 multi-syllable words page xiv.

© 2010 Sarah K Major

In **here**

not there,

and I **hear**

with my ear.

There they go to see

their fir tree!

My stew isn't **new!**

I **knew** it!

It's old!

The skunk left a **scent.**

The **cent** is round.

Selina **sent** me there!

Our dog went out

an **hour** ago.

Fingermapping: Section 6 letter clusters page xiii.

© 2010 Sarah K Major

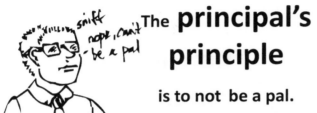

The **principal's principle** is to not be a pal.

The coat is made of **coarse** cloth. Of **course** it itches.

The **vane** is in the lane.

This **vein** is in my arm.

She's **vain** until she's in the rain!

Wait! I need the **weight** of 8 sleighs!

The **capitol** building is in the **capital** city of Alabama.

Colin the **Colonel** ate a **kernel** of corn with kermit and Nel.

Fingermapping: Section 6 letter clusters page xiii and Section 8 multi-syllable words page xiv.

© 2010 Sarah K Major   128